TWILIGHT OF THE SAINTS:

Biblical Christianity & Civil Religion in America

Robert D. Linder & Richard V. Pierard

InterVarsity Press
Downers Grove, Illinois
60515

InterVarsity Press is the book publishing
division of Inter-Varsity Christian
Fellowship, a student movement active
on campus at hundreds of
universities, colleges and schools of nursing.
For information about local and
regional activities, write IVCF,
233 Langdon St., Madison, WI 53703.

ISBN 0-87784-505-0
Library of Congress
Catalog Card Number: 77-002680

Printed in the United States of America

To our parents

So put away all malice and all guile and
insincerity and envy and all slander.
Like newborn babes, long for the pure spiritual
milk, that by it you may grow up to
salvation; for you have tasted the kindness
of the Lord.

Come to him, to that living stone, rejected by
men but in God's sight chosen and
precious; and like living stones be yourselves
built into a spiritual house, to be a holy
priesthood, to offer spiritual sacrifices
acceptable to God through Jesus Christ. . . .

But you are a chosen race, a royal
priesthood, a holy nation, God's own people,
that you may declare the wonderful deeds
of him who called you out of darkness
into his marvelous light.
(1 Peter 2:1-5, 9)

Now, those that ponder these things, their
spirits are grieved in the midst of their
bodies;—the visions of their heads
trouble them. They looked for other things
from them that professed Christ; but the
summer is ended, and the harvest is past, and
we are not refreshed.
(John Owen, 1652)

With malice toward none, with charity
for all, with firmness in the right as God gives
us to see the right, let us strive on to
finish the work we are in, to bind up the
nation's wounds, to care for him who
shall have borne the battle and for his widow
and his orphan, to do all which may
achieve and cherish a just and lasting peace
among ourselves and with all nations.
(Abraham Lincoln, Second Inaugural Address,
March 4, 1865)

PREFACE

There are two important things which the authors of this book have in common—we are citizens of the United States of America and we profess an evangelical Christian faith. One is the result of our natural birth, the other of a conscious choice made in response to the preaching of the gospel. More than anything else, these two factors have shaped our lives and underlie the thinking in the pages which follow. We painfully realize that both the American and the evangelical traditions contain a mixture of the positive and negative, the profound and the banal, but we make no apologies for either our national or spiritual background.

In our judgment, among the most valuable features of the American character are its revolutionary heritage and its openness to change. This country was founded by people who refused to be bound by the dictates of custom and procedure, and who sought a richer, fuller existence in the New World across the sea. In their new home they questioned established authority and rebelled against the tyranny of king and Parliament. They created political institutions that would be eternally subject to the control and correction of those who were being governed. This explains why Americans historically have been suspicious of movements which stressed unquestioning and/or unqualified submission to political authority and why they willingly shed their blood when necessary to preserve their liberties.

We identify fully with this aspect of our national tradition, but, as Christians, we would add that God has also freed us from the elemental forces of this present world which seek to hold us in spiritual bondage. Both our American and Christian heritages have implanted in our beings a critical faculty, a penchant to question things as they are and to measure them by higher, even transcendent standards, for example, the natural rights which all people possess as created beings and beyond that the eternal laws of God as set down in the Bible. Thus, we have an inner compulsion to subject our society and all its institutions to a continual process of review.

It goes without saying that there always will be tension between our loyalty to Christ and that which we owe to the various institutions of society, such as family, school, employer, church congregation and above all the state. The task we have as believers is to order our priorities so that Christ always occupies the pre-eminent position. To permit any of our loyalties to have a place alongside or above Christ is defined by Scripture in no uncertain terms as idolatry. The state, because it is the only institution that encompasses all of the particular inhabitants of a society, has a perverse tendency to demand the final allegiance of its citizens. Hence, Christians frequently find themselves having to resist the claims of the state.

A long historical tradition of conflict between commitment to Christ and the unlawful demands of the political ruler stretches from the Roman Empire to twentieth-century Nazi Germany and Soviet Russia. In the modern democratic state where the government is responsible to its citizens and its absolutistic tendencies are accordingly checked, this should not be a serious problem; but even such a state may maneuver itself into a position of requiring more from its citizens than it ought by espousing some form of civil religion. This phenomenon often leads to a conflict of loyalties, and Christians need to be informed about both the creative potential and the demonic tendencies of civil religion. The recent Bicentennial observance has made us keenly aware of the necessity to engage in a critical re-evaluation of the institutional forms of American civil religion.

Since we are professional historians, it is only natural that we would want to know how and why civil religion became so deeply ingrained in the American psyche. As Christians we feel compelled to ask still other questions: What is this civil faith? Can it and genuine Christianity coexist peacefully? What should the attitude of the followers of Jesus Christ be toward it? Thus, we have decided to undertake an examination of the American civic faith in order to determine how we as Christians should relate to it. What follows is the result of our quest.

As we begin the third century of our national existence, we have a professing Christian at the helm of the country who openly acknowledges that he has been "born again." It is our desire that he will allow his conscience to be informed by the New Testament, thereby enabling American evangelicals to rally behind him, both for the benefit of our country and the ongoing interests of the kingdom of God. If President Jimmy Carter is faithful to his persuasion, and American Christians are prepared to give him the spiritual backing and loving correction that he needs to fulfill his constitutional duties properly, then there may be hope for the survival of this nation as a positive moral force in the world. However, we are deeply concerned that civil religion may continue to serve as a mask for the more unpleasant side of the American character and be instrumental in leading the nation in the direction of dictatorship—perhaps even fascism. Whether civil religion can play a positive, corrective role in our society very clearly remains to be seen.

In conclusion, we want to thank our families who patiently endured closed study doors and periods of intense concentration on the subject at hand, and Jean Ann Linder who typed the final draft of this manuscript in its entirety out of Christian conviction and love for her husband but little else!

Robert D. Linder
Department of History
Kansas State University

Richard V. Pierard
Department of History
Indiana State University

1
THE HARVEST IS PAST & WE ARE NOT REFRESHED

Documentary films of World War 2 often feature one of America's best-loved singers, Kate Smith, belting out what became one of the most popular tunes of that era—"God Bless America." Many Americans over age forty can recall fervently singing these words during the war years:

> While the storm clouds gather far across the sea,
> Let us swear allegiance to a land that's free;
> Let us all be grateful for a land so fair,
> As we raise our voices in a solemn prayer.
>
> God bless America, land that I love,
> Stand beside her and guide her
> Through the night with a light from above:
> From the mountains, to the prairies
> To the oceans white with foam,
> God bless America, my home sweet home.[1]

Even today this hymn of simultaneous supplication and affirmation of God's special watch-care of America is sung widely in the churches, schools and political halls of the nation. As countless thousands waft its stirring words and melody over the length and breadth of the land, they engage in what many scholars describe as *civil religion*.

What is civil religion? How is is it expressed in American

life today? At what points does it appeal to the majority of Americans in order to furnish the social and moral cohesiveness which many of its proponents argue is its most useful and desirable characteristic? Perhaps a few illustrations—of which "God Bless America" is one—will provide the most helpful background for a discussion of these and related questions.

Blending Piety and Patriotism   Another example of this blending of patriotism and piety into one emotional-conceptual experience is the habitual use of God-words by American politicians, especially presidents. For instance, former President Richard M. Nixon addressed the nation from the White House on prime time television on April 29, 1974, in an effort to convince the American people that the release of twelve hundred pages of transcripts of presidential conversations would settle the Watergate matter once and for all in his favor. Unfortunately, the speech describing the heavily edited documents was full of partial and outright lies. The complete tapes later released demonstrated that the former president told at least seven major untruths during the course of his remarks that evening. Sitting at his desk with a picture of his family on one side, a bust of Abraham Lincoln on the other and an American flag in the background, Mr. Nixon ended the speech with these words:

I deeply believe that America is the hope of the world, and I know that in the quality and wisdom of the leadership America gives lies the only hope for millions of people all over the world, that they can live their lives in peace and freedom. We must be worthy of that hope, in every sense of the word. Tonight, I ask for your prayers to help me in everything that I do throughout the days of my Presidency to be worthy of their hopes and of yours. God bless America and God bless each and everyone of you.[2]

In doing so, the former president conformed to the expectations of at least one political glossary which answered the question, "Who is God?" with, "God is a word which appears in the closing paragraph of a politician's speech."[3] It is worth noting that these pious sentiments were voiced by an individual whom the White House tapes have revealed as an essentially profane man whose foul language and arrogant views showed little trace of a religiously informed conscience or a regard for humanity.

The man who ran against Nixon for the presidency in 1972 likewise engaged in acts of public religiosity. For example, in the summer of that year George McGovern visited the predominantly black Community Methodist Church in New York City's Harlem district and delivered the Sunday morning sermon. On that occasion he also received the endorsement of the church's distinguished pastor, the Reverend William M. James. Before McGovern spoke the congregation joined in a hymn:

The voice of God is calling
It summons unto men:
As once he spake in Zion
So now he speaks again:
Whom shall I send to succor
My people in their need?
Whom shall I send to loosen
The bonds of shame and greed?[4]

Whom shall I send? The Reverend Mr. James responded categorically to that question in his introduction of the Democratic candidate: "We are proud to have Senator McGovern with us this morning. . . . History has brought him; the God of history has brought him to lead a crusade for the benefit of all mankind."[5]

The candidate from South Dakota opened his address with one of his favorite biblical texts: "The Spirit of the Lord is upon me, because he has anointed me to preach good news to the poor. He has sent me to proclaim release to the captives and recovering of sight to the blind, to set at liberty those who are oppressed, to proclaim the acceptable year of the Lord" (Lk. 4:18-19). McGovern then expounded the agenda that he felt the nation so desperately needed to hear by reviewing his recent campaign proposals.

In a similar manner this propensity to marry religious and political sentiments is often found in the adoration of the American flag. The United States is one of the few nations of the world where the flag has religious as well as political significance, especially for evangelical Christians. Members of this group, more than any other segment of the population, are inclined to have a religious experience when they view the national banner. Thus, one well-known evangelical leader unashamedly writes a "love letter to a flag," while another person confesses that the stars and stripes remind him not only of his country but also of his Savior. Others who view the flag praise God that they are Christians and Americans, and thankfully "repeat the Pledge of Allegiance to my God and Country." Desecration of the flag usually evokes greater indignation and emotional reaction on the part of Christians than does the use of God's name in vain. They look the other way when the cross, the symbol of Christianity, is burned, but fly into a rage when someone touches a match to the flag, the symbol of the nation.[6]

There are many other examples of this impulse to blend piety and patriotism, religious and political feelings in American life. Note the presence in American Christian hymnbooks of songs like "The Star-Spangled Banner" and "America the Beautiful." Study the inaugural and farewell addresses of the presidents of the United States. Notice, as nearly all Christian visitors from other lands do, the presence of the American flag in church sanctuaries. Moreover, there are certain sacral days on which Americans celebrate political and semipolitical events with religious language, acts and fervor: Memorial Day, the Fourth of July and Thanksgiving Day. Christians and members of other religious faiths usually sanction and participate in the celebration of these national holidays cum holy days.

Religiosity is often present at political and civic functions in the form of invocations and benedictions. The more religiously plural a community, the more carefully balanced the program must appear in terms of the religious affiliations of those who do the invoking and give the benedictions. Recent presidential inaugurations featuring prayers by representatives of each of the four major religious faiths of the nation—Protestant, Roman Catholic, Jewish and Eastern Orthodox—illustrate well this sort of approach to giving the Deity his due.

The God-and-country mix intrudes into other facets of American life as well. The Liberty Bowl football extravaganza sponsors a half-time show which blends religious and political sentiments. Many professional soldiers spend their lives worshiping in a generalized "Army church" which instills in them both patriotism and religious principles in such a manner that neither ever really gets in the way of the other—as the case of the late General George S. Patton, Jr. demonstrates so well.[7] Those who occasionally remain awake late enough to watch the sign-off on their local television station may observe a film clip provided by a major denomination, the final shot of which is a camera sweep from the American flag to the cross-crowned church steeple. The symbolism is clear.

But perhaps the most persistent reminders of the presence of civil religion in the United States are the phrase "one nation under God" in the Pledge of Allegiance, the official national motto "In God We Trust" and the popular "If My People" prayer movement which subliminally communicates the notion that America is the New Israel. What, then, are the implications of these various religio-political affirmations?

First, the "one nation under God" statement raises the age-old God and Caesar issue with all of its concomitant questions. When Christ responded to the Pharisees' and Herodians' attempt to entrap him with "Render therefore to Caesar the things that are Caesar's, and to God the things that are God's" (Mt. 22: 15-22), he was addressing this problem of the fusing of ultimate loyalties. Christ's teaching on this point, as well as other New Testament statements that the highest loyalty of a Christian is always to God, makes it necessary to ask certain questions about the "one nation under God" declaration. Does such a concept blur the line drawn by Christ between God and Caesar? What does it mean to be one nation under God? If the assertion is made in a theocratic-political sense, has such a nation ever existed since the time of ancient Israel?

Second, "In God We Trust"—on American coins since the Civil War and the national motto since 1956—also poses questions for prophetic biblical Christianity. Is there a parallel between the action of Roman Emperor Constantine I placing both Christian and pagan mottoes on his coinage following his conversion to Christianity in the early fourth century and the fact that United States money contains both religious and nonreligious symbols and slogans? What does the phrase "in God we trust" mean? Does America as a nation, in fact, trust in God? If this is actually the case, why does it spend such vast amounts of money annually on military hardware? Has it ever trusted in God? Who is the "God" to whom this trust supposedly is directed, the God of Christianity or some other deity? Does such an affirmation tend to sanction the status quo and mute the prophetic voice of the Christian faith?

Third, the "If My People" prayer endeavor and similar ventures during the Bicentennial observance that concentrated on national intercession also raise important questions concerning the relationship between civil religion and biblical Christianity. These questions center around the identification of America as "God's New Israel," an elect nation which has inherited the premises and promises of God once made to Israel of old before the Christian era. The essence of this movement is the popular application of 2 Chronicles 7:14 to the United States: "If my people who are called by my name humble themselves, and pray and seek my face, and turn from their wicked ways, then I will hear from heaven, and will forgive their sin and heal their land."[8] To whom is this statement addressed and for what purpose? What is its significance for American Christians and for the nation? Is the United States the present-day equivalent of ancient Israel? If applicable to the United States, does it call all Americans or only the Christians of the country to repentance? What is the purpose of this call and what results may be expected if the conditions are met?

What Is Civil Religion?   All of the foregoing describe various manifestations of civil religion and some of the accompanying problems. But what exactly is civil religion? As a matter of fact, not all scholars agree upon a single definition of the term and a few do not accept its existence at all. On the other hand it is fair to say that there is a rather widespread and growing use of the term to conceptualize an existent reality which only recently has become the focal point for critical analysis by an increasing number of historians, political scientists, sociologists and theologians. Thus, it appears that a working definition can be formulated which will facilitate a meaningful discussion of the relationship of biblical Christianity and civil religion in modern America.

Briefly stated, *civil religion* is the use of consensus religious sentiments, concepts and symbols by the state—either directly or indirectly, consciously or unconsciously—for its own political purposes. These purposes may be noble or debased, depending upon the type of civil religion (priestly or prophetic) and the historical context. It involves mixing traditional religion with national life until it is impossible to distinguish between the two, and usually leads to a blurring of religion and patriotism and of religious values with national values. In the case of American civil religion it is a rather elaborate matrix of beliefs and practices born of the nation's historic experience and constituting the only real religion of millions of its citizens.[9]

Sociologist Robert N. Bellah, who in 1967 revived the use of the term civil religion and stimulated widespread debate and discussion of the concept, asserts that "few have realized that there actually exists alongside of and rather clearly differentiated from the churches an elaborate and well-institutionalized civil religion in America."[10] The reason it exists, he argues, is that every community is based on a sense of the sacred and requires a context of higher meaning. In the United States civil religion often superficially looks like Christianity, overlaps it at some points, appropriates much of its terminology, but is different from it in its essentials. Unlike biblical Christianity, civil religion is a relativistic and somewhat amorphous phenomenon. In other words it is not to be identified strictly with any particular denomination or faith, but rather it is an extraecclesiastical religion which serves the patriotic cause of illuminating the national identity.

Civil religion expresses itself in American life in a myriad of ways, as the illustrations at the beginning of this chapter point out. In addition, the Declaration of Independence, the Constitution and perhaps Abraham Lincoln's Gettysburg Address are the sacred documents of the civil faith. Civil religionists are inclined to think of every war in which America engages as a righteous conflict, and of the American way of life as synonymous with God's way. Public schools often serve as the chief vehicles for inculcating and celebrating this national faith.

Perhaps the key to modern American civil faith is the role of the president as "high priest." The chief executive—using bland religious terms such as faith, belief, sacrifice, hope and spirit—projects the image of a priest comforting his people, assuring them of their basic goodness and striving to enhance their self-esteem. Ray Price, a 1968 Nixon advisor and speechwriter, ably analyzed this religious-mythic aura which surrounds any president:

> People identify with a President in a way they do with no other public figure. Potential Presidents are measured against an ideal that's a combination of leading man, God, father, hero, pope, king, with maybe just a touch of the avenging Furies thrown in. They want him to be larger than life, a living legend, and yet quintessentially human; someone to be held up to their children as a model; some-

one to be cherished by themselves as a revered member of the family, in somewhat the same way in which peasant families pray to the icon in the corner. Reverence goes where power is.[11]

Numerous evangelical Christians in the United States identify with many of the foregoing illustrations of participatory civil religion by assuming that America is in some unique sense a Christian nation, therefore making it ipso facto different from and better than all others. They view the Constitution and American system of government as Christian and believe that evangelical principles are the foundation and hope of the nation. Moreover, they see the United States as having a special role in world history and take for granted that it has been the focal point for the spread of Christianity and the American way to the remainder of the world. Given the American historical experience and this sort of conditioned world view, the purpose of God and the national purpose easily become one.

Failure of the Puritan Experiment   In an earlier era but in a similar setting another large body of godly people had such an outlook and hope for their nation. These were the seventeenth-century English Puritans who under the leadership of disciplined, dedicated and pious men, sought a further reformation of the Church of England which in their view had been arrested when only half done. They not only wanted to preach the gospel to all of their fellow countrymen so that the elect would respond and embrace Christ but also to redeem what they understood to be the outward face of religion, namely, the institutions, discipline and worship of the church. At first they tried to bring this about within the existing ecclesiastical structure of the Anglican establishment, but eventually they took up arms to complete the English Reformation by means of public authority.

In so doing, the Puritans developed an apocalyptic view of their place in history commensurate with the religious and political goals they envisioned for their country. The

Puritans thought of human history as the field in which God gathered his saints, saving those whom he had predestined from the fate which all deserved and imparting to those elect ones some knowledge of his will. After a period of spiritual decline and stagnation during the centuries following the conversion of Constantine, the Puritans saw an upswing in true godliness with the coming of the Protestant Reformation in the sixteenth century. More and more people turned to Christ, and country after country was touched by the spiritual revival sweeping the Western world. But it was the Puritan who stood on the crest of the movement and it was England which seemed to be the chosen nation of God to fulfill his purposes in the world. It was this longing to be the instruments of God's will in history that drove the Puritans to attempt to establish a national church purified of all spiritual dross and Roman aberrations. This assurance that they were cooperating with God and moving toward a preordained victory supplied the élan for the Puritan-Parliamentarian triumph over the forces of the monarchy in the English Civil War, 1642-1649. This same thirst for theocracy and strident millennialism led Oliver Cromwell and his associates to attempt to establish a godly commonwealth in which the saints ruled the country as a "nation under God."[12]

Alas, frustration was the fate that awaited the Puritans of midseventeenth-century England. They were a minority of the population and soon found it extremely difficult to govern the majority who did not share their religious and political views. Even worse, the saints fell out among themselves. They differed considerably over the form of government and the implementation of public policy. Some were political conservatives, others radicals. Some wanted a national church that was basically presbyterian, others supported congregational church government, while still others desired a modified episcopal form of polity for a truly reformed Church of England. Some backed Cromwell's policy of religious toleration, others did not. Others complained about his foreign policy and criticized his failure to bring about a thorough moral reformation of English society in general.

By 1652 the Puritan movement was rent asunder by dispute after dispute within its own ranks. More and more saints withdrew their support from Cromwell who by the early 1650s had become a benevolent dictator. Disillusionment set in and discontent was rife. A crisis engulfed the Commonwealth from which it never recovered. In 1658 Cromwell died and two years later the monarchy was restored in England. The distinguished Oxford don and Puritan intellectual Dr. John Owen originally had been full of millennial hope as well as a staunch supporter of Cromwell and the new English Commonwealth. However, by 1652, he too was frustrated and disillusioned. Listen to his analysis of the situation:

> What now, by the lusts of men, is the state of things? Say some, there is no gospel at all; some others, if there be, you have nothing to do with it;—some say, lo, here is Christ; others, lo, there;—some make religion a colour for one thing; some for another;—say some, the magistrate must not support the gospel; say others, the gospel must subvert the magistrate. . . . If you will have the gospel, say some, down with the ministers of it . . . and if you will have light, take care that you may have ignorance and darkness. . . . Now, those that ponder these things, their spirits are grieved in the midst of their bodies;—the visions of their heads trouble them. They looked for other things from them that professed Christ; *but the summer is ended and the harvest is past, and we are not refreshed.* [13]

Many evangelical Christians in the crisis-ridden America of the 1960s and 1970s well might echo Owen's lament. What has happened to the great American experiment which owes so much of its impetus and direction to the same Puritan movement transplanted to colonial America? What happened to the dream of the early American Puritans to establish a biblical commonwealth which would serve as a moral example to all the world? What has become of the hopes and dreams of the American evangelicals who once composed the religious mainstream of the nation and who believed that it was both possible and desirable to make the United States a "city upon a hill"? Are evangelicals today, in the face of the present crisis, as frustrated and disillusioned as was Owen with the great Puritan experiment in midseventeenth-century England?[14] Would they say with him: "The summer is ended, and the harvest is past, and we are not refreshed"?

The American Crisis   In many ways the situation in America today is even more dangerous and critical than it was in the England of Owen's time. This has been particularly true since the assassination of President John F. Kennedy and the ensuing events of the 1960s. The history of the United States since 1963 reads like a grand gothic horror tale told on a national scale. Historians in the future undoubtedly will have a difficult time putting what has happened in the past decade and a half in an understandable perspective for coming generations of Americans—if there are any.[15]

Most people over twenty-five can recall the shock and horror of November 22, 1963, when news of the Kennedy assassination flashed across the television screens of the nation. It seemed incredible that such a villainous act could have taken place in an orderly and peaceful society like the United States. And it was followed by equally traumatic political killings and attempted killings: Senator Robert F. Kennedy and Dr. Martin Luther King, Jr., in 1968; Governor George Wallace in 1972; and President Gerald R. Ford in 1975. The course of events since 1963 has so twisted the American psyche that political assassination is now an accepted part of national life—so much so that the press and people already have steeled themselves mentally for the next attempt.

And there was the Vietnam War—a war which seemed never to end, one which left deep and lasting scars on the nation as it divided friends and families. It was a conflict which destroyed both Vietnamese villages and American confidence in its political leaders with the My Lai Massacre in 1968 and the shooting of Kent State University students in 1970. It was a struggle which cost the United States thousands of lives, billions of dollars and millions of gallons of irreplaceable fuel and other energy sources. The fact that it ended with a whimper rather than a bang served to leave thousands of Americans restless and dissatisfied. Moreover, the Vietnamese refugees who streamed into this country in 1975 remain highly visible as a great object lesson of imperialism coming home to roost.

But during those years from 1963 to the present there was also the immensely impressive feat of putting a human on the moon in 1969. Who can forget that accomplishment—a staggering display of skill and technology achieved at equally staggering costs! However, the jaded younger generation could only comment: "How come it took so long?" And the tax-weary older generation could only ask: "What value is it?"

Add to all this the deaths of three former presidents in those years: Dwight D. Eisenhower in 1969, Harry S. Truman in 1972 and Lyndon B. Johnson in 1973. Then Americans had no elder statesmen to whom they could turn for guidance and perspective. Most would acknowledge that there was a certain irony and an infinite sadness attached to the fact that the only living ex-president in the year of the celebration of the Bicentennial was a man named Richard M. Nixon.

Moreover, there were the dangerous Arab-Israeli Wars of 1967 and 1973. The world came close to a major conflict between the super powers in those years, as it was touch and go in the embassies for several weeks in both conflicts. Many historians still regard the Middle East situation as the most dangerous on the globe—the potential Armageddon of a future world conflagration. But perhaps the most fearful fact about the Middle East is that most Americans apparently know little and care less about what happens there.

In the 1960s the modern civil rights movement in America saw the fulfillment of many of its objectives, but at the same time it was a period of turmoil and significant increase in crime and violence. The seriousness of the situation was noted by then private citizen Nixon in a 1967 *Reader's Digest* article containing more than its share of irony entitled "What Has Happened to America?"[16] After noting the slippage of moral and legal standards, denouncing the current wave of violence, acknowledging the need for more social mobility for blacks, and calling for a new candor in dealing with the growing problem of lawlessness in America, Mr. Nixon penned: "To heal the wounds that have torn the nation asunder, to re-establish respect for law and the principles that have been the source of America's growth and greatness will require the example of leaders in every walk of American life."[17]

Concomitant with the war in Vietnam and the civil rights movement, and in many ways growing out of them, was the student unrest of the 1960s. Students demonstrated and rioted and in turn were beaten and shot by police. Often campuses were disrupted with sit-ins as radical students issued demands for sweeping changes in the university structure. Education in some ways became more humane and in others more mediocre. Most important and enduring, the educational drift and anti-intellectualism generated by the campus unrest of the 1960s still dominate many universities, public educational systems and state legislatures.

In the midst of this turmoil, Americans discovered that all was not well with their environment. Pollution problems came to the fore—most of them yet unresolved. Tragically, the realization that the environment had to be saved was not shared by millions of Americans struggling to make a living or simply trying to keep themselves and their families alive. They became the unwitting allies of those in the business community who wanted to make one more dollar before government controls cut back their profits to a more modest level.

And then there was the Watergate affair! What historian will be able to convey faithfully and believably the agony of the American nation in the years 1973-74? It was as if the country had a death wish, as a time of presidential lying and cover-ups shook the republic to its very foundations. Fortunately, the foundations were sound and held in the tempest. But, in the wake of Watergate came more revelations of misconduct and immorality in the highest echelons of the national government. The FBI and CIA scandals disclosed that federal agencies long trusted by the American people had abridged and violated the constitutional rights of thousands of the nation's citizens. The situation was not helped as the slop-bucket morality of several recent presidents and congressmen came to light via presidential papers, tapes, and talkative ex-mistresses and girl friends.

Along with these upheavals in national life has occurred a critical energy shortage which was accentuated by the devastating winter of 1977 and concurrent raging inflation and economic depression. Americans appear to be living in a fool's paradise as they are lulled to sleep with faint assurances that somebody someplace is doing something about the energy crisis, inflation and unemployment. In the meantime the price of gasoline creeps steadily toward the dollar per gallon mark, inflation has become a way of life, and the reality that millions of Americans in Detroit and New York are daily degraded by unemployment and welfare hardly concerns their fellow citizens living in more prosperous sections of the nation. Some experts say there will be no more gasoline by the end of the 1980s; and if the nation experiences full economic recovery soon, its present energy sources may dry up even more quickly.

In assessing the happenings of 1975, Hugh Sidey of *Time* magazine noted that it was a year lacking in clear sentiment, definitive events, towering leaders and firm direction for the country. He concluded, "Above all, it was a year in which Viet Nam and Watergate ended, a time of transition from an anguished era to a future not yet clearly discerned."[18]

But all of this leaves aside any direct attention to the moral and spiritual decay which many evangelical Christian leaders feel has taken place in America over the past fifteen years, despite the fact that there have been signs of widespread spiritual renewal during the same period.[19] Characteristic of this sort of concern by Christian spokespersons are remarks made not long ago by the country's leading evangelist, Billy Graham, and distinguished evangelical theologian, Carl F. H. Henry.

Speaking in the Landon Lecture series on public issues at Kansas State University on March 4, 1974, Dr. Graham dwelt on the crisis of modern America. After surveying various aspects of the political and economic problems confronting the nation he turned to what he considered the greatest crisis of America today—moral and spiritual decadence. In so doing he gravely observed: "I am often asked, 'Is America at the crossroads?' No, America is not at a crossroads! We have already passed the crossroads. We have already made a decision. We made a decision a long time ago to abandon God and go our own way.... We chose the road to secularism, hedonism, materialism, and moral permissiveness."[20]

More recently Dr. Henry expressed his views on America as a country in transition in the religious journal *Interpretation*. Like Graham, he acknowledged the fact that the late 1960s and early 1970s was a time of evangelical resurgence in the Western world, and that this was encouraging. But he also was deeply troubled over the loss of biblical values in national life:

> There are hopeful breakthroughs and sporadic gains at radically secular frontiers, but this is clearly something less than national repentance and renewal. The arena of intellectual and cultural concerns is determinedly non-evangelical. The social and political practices of our time derive less and less inspiration from biblical ideas, and our civilization will not long survive this bankrupting loss. The state of the nation spiritually is generally not good.[21]

Perhaps as well as anyone, historian Barbara Tuchman expressed the relationship of the moral to the political in the course of her analysis of the meaning of the Watergate hearings. In so doing she reduced the political scandal to ultimate moral terms. She was struck by the lack of a sense of wrongdoing in the Nixon people:

> The witnesses' casual contempt for society's rules, including the Ninth Commandment—'Thou shalt not bear false witness against thy neighbor'—was so untroubled as almost to suggest ignorance. One wondered, where did they go to school? Who were their parents, their teachers and pastors? Did all of them somehow skip what used to be called Civics in the eighth grade?
>
> In formulating that question one begins to understand the nature of the tragedy. These men are not peculiar to the Nixon White House (although it evidently attracted a high concentration of the raw arrogance of the parvenu). They are what has happened to America and to our time. The same contempt for the rules is visible in street people who relieve themselves on doorsteps, and muggers who murder without a blush, and Mets fans who treat a visiting team throughout with howling hostility and swarm like a lynch mob over the field, trampling on people in their eagerness to wreck and vandalize.... Without conventional restraints man becomes dangerous or unpleasant whether in the White House or in Shea Stadium.[22]

There is the growing feeling among close observers of the national scene that America has entered a time of trial such as it has not experienced since its Civil War more than a century ago. As in the period of the tragic war between the states, so these are "times which try men's souls!" The supreme irony is that in the middle of all this the United States was celebrating its Bicentennial. Like the Puritans of old England—whose experiment did not endure nearly as long as that of their American brethren—many evangelical Christians are beginning to share the feeling of frustration that John Owen had expressed.

The New Pluralism and the Old Identity   As Americans are now in the Bicentennial era (1975-1989, when the parallel events associated with the founding of the country will be celebrated), they are more polarized and more pluralistic than at any other time in the nation's history. The polarity is as severe as it was in the Civil War period. However, today there are more issues and identities which sharply divide the people of the country into hostile factions: not only traditional politics but also race and ethnicity, religion, sex, regionalism, urban and rural allegiances, culture and counterculture, socioeconomic class and age. It is little wonder that one author entitled his history of the 1960s *Coming Apart.*[23]

This new era of polarity and pluralism in national life has created strains which have driven many thinking Americans to renew the quest for national identity and purpose. The old sense of identity and purpose of the nineteenth century has vanished like the evangelical consensus upon which it rested. It is no longer self-evident that America is God's chosen vessel to spread evangelical Christianity and democracy to the remainder of the world. The Protestant ethic in morality and economics is no longer the norm of the land; the fervor of evangelical religion no longer spawns surging moral reform crusades and benevolent associations to purify the nation and redeem the world; the "Battle Hymn of the Republic" no longer stirs the cockles of patriotic hearts with its message of millennial faith and optimistic conviction; and many have the growing feeling that indeed "the summer is ended, and the harvest is past, and we are not refreshed."[24]

The place at which the American nation stands in the 1970s following the Vietnam War is poignantly described in the closing words of David Halberstam's widely heralded *The Best and the Brightest:*

> The inability of the Americans to impose their will on Vietnam had been answered in 1968, yet the leadership of the country had not been able to adjust our goals to that failure. And so the war went on, tearing at this country; a sense of numbness seemed to replace an earlier anger.

There was, Americans were finding, no light at the end of the tunnel, only greater darkness.[25]

As the United States entered the decade of the 1970s, it was politically and socially divided. Moreover, the strains of the Vietnam conflict accentuated what many scholars had pointed out previously—America was now a highly pluralistic nation of greatly diversified peoples. This was especially true in religion, where by the midtwentieth century it was clear that there was a large non-Christian minority—supported by many Protestants—who were not committed to the American religious heritage in the form in which it had developed over the course of American history.

In the broadest terms, America had become deeply divided politically, culturally and religiously. It was adrift with little or no sense of national identity or purpose. From a more narrowly political and not necessarily Christian point of view, Boston campaign consultant John P. Martilla observed early in 1976: "America has lost its faith in its institutions. ... It's lost its sense of political common purpose."[26]

In a more specifically Christian context, political leaders like evangelical Congressman John B. Anderson of Illinois have come to similar conclusions. In his 1975 book *Vision and Betrayal in America*, Anderson discussed the immediate past and the future of the country from a Christian perspective, and like many other contemporary observers noted the present crisis:

> The collapse of American *ideals* from which the nation has received its inspiration, the failure of American *institutions* to operate effectively and deliberately, and the betrayal of *individuals* assigned positions of leadership in government have all come at once. Weakness in any of these three areas is bad enough. But it has been our unfortunate lot to experience them all at the same moment.[27]

The Bicentennial Many politicans and not a few prominent figures from the religious community regarded the celebration of the Bicentennial as a vehicle for drawing the nation together once again. The year 1976 was characterized by a bewildering array of approaches—from the shallow and the perverse to the reflective and the noble. For many it was a grand opportunity to make a fast buck. Stars and stripes cupcakes appeared, huge Bicentennial advertising campaigns were undertaken and one headline in a local Concord, Massachusetts newspaper proclaimed: "The Tourists Are Coming!"[28]

On the other hand, many seriously attempted to celebrate the nation's two-hundredth birthday with dignity and meaning. One somewhat critical observer pointed out, "There is nothing like a wretched backdrop to stimulate interest in a national celebration; the worse the times, the greater the need for diversion and self-congratulation."[29] In a more positive vein, Governor Richard D. Lamm of Colorado pleaded:

> As we move toward our Bicentennial year let us re-examine what it means to be Americans. The value of being an American is not measured by having two cars in every garage and a color television set. Our progress as a people cannot be measured by garbage compactors, B-1 bombers and plastic flowers. It is measured by our continued right to live and work in equality and freedom, being judged only on our ability. Our country is great not because we have great leaders but because we have a great people, people who overcame adversity, poverty, prejudice and handicaps of all kinds.[30]

There were many similar calls for sober thought about national allegiance, solidarity, security, values, purpose and meaning. In short, although the crass and commercial elements were abundantly present, there were also those leaders who tried to make the Bicentennial celebration an occasion to pull a badly divided nation together again.

Not all Americans responded favorably to this twentieth-century "serious call to a devout and civic life." Large numbers of individuals in various minority groups questioned the propriety of celebrating an event in which they felt they had no stake. Many of the poor and dispossessed simply did not participate. Some evangelicals struggled mightily with various options vis-à-vis the Bicentennial: ignore it, celebrate part of it or join wholeheartedly in the festivities.[31]

Manifestations of civil religion became a part of this Bicentennial effort of the American people to pull themselves together. In many ways this was natural since the mythologizing of the American experience has been integral to American nationalism and self-understanding. In 1976 civil religion—not Christianity—was the rallying point for those who felt that a common faith was the major ingredient needed to cultivate a new national consciousness and cohesiveness. In other words many leaders felt that the answer to the strains of polarity and pluralism and the answer to the new search for national identity and destiny was the cultivation of civil faith. The values of civil religion were substituted for the values of the evangelical consensus of the nineteenth century in order to restore a sense of moral order and unite the country in a common religious outlook.[32]

Questions for Christians   What does all of this mean to the individual Christian as he or she ponders the political future? How is the present social-political crisis in America relevant to the preaching of the gospel? In what ways and how intimately is the future of historic evangelical Christianity in America tied up with the future of America itself?

In order to answer these important questions, it is necessary to raise others for thought and consideration. First and foremost, every evangelical—consciously or unconsciously—will have to address the issue: Is America worth saving? If so, why, and if not, why not? In this connection the political health of the nation becomes a major factor. How important are the Bill of Rights and the ideals of freedom for the ongoing work of Christ in the United States? Is it true that America is a land of opportunity to better one's lot in life, a place where all people enjoy political and religious freedom, a veritable base camp for supporting a worldwide missionary movement, a country which permits the full and free expression of the Christian faith? Or is all of this a myth? Or worse yet, are these ideals of the American past which have now been lost?

Second, what is the responsibility of the individual Christian and of groups of Christians (churches, denominations, interdenominational agencies) in this time of national crisis? What is the proper relationship of Christians and Christianity to the state? How can believers distinguish between responsible patriotism and irresponsible nationalism, and what should constitute effective discipleship?

Third, during a period of turmoil such as the present, how can Christians avoid being used or manipulated by the state for its own purposes? Can they cooperate with the regime to help resolve the current crisis without being co-opted by the state through a generalized civil religion? Is it possible, or even desirable, for Christians to embrace American civil religion while at the same time maintaining their primary commitment to Jesus Christ? At what points is it possible for them to join with non-Christians as cobelligerents (but not necessarily as allies, to utilize Francis Schaeffer's useful distinction) in the new quest for national identity and values, and when must evangelical Christians in particular withhold support in order to avoid compromising the gospel?[33]

These are tough problems. A number of them will be addressed directly in this volume, while others will be touched upon only indirectly. Ultimately each Christian believer will have to seek out his or her own answers to them. On the other hand a lack of consensus among this generation of evangelical Christians in America could be fatal—at least in terms of national survival. It is that serious![34]

More bluntly and directly in terms of civil religion, American Christians need to reflect upon and respond to the following questions. First, is there a difference between civil religion and Christianity—between civil deism and biblical faith? If so, are the two in any sense and under any circumstances compatible? Second, have evangelical leaders who have supported civil religion in the past been duped or has their support been legitimate and biblical? Third, can organized society exist without some sort of religious glue like civil religion? Or, can biblical Christianity inform national values and the national lifestyle without participating in a largely non-Christian civil religion? Finally, is democracy possible without a biblical base upon which to rest? If so, does this mean that if there is to be civil religion in a democratic society, it must be a biblically-oriented civil faith? If not, does this mean the death knell for democracy in the United States?

The problems and the prospects of America in the latter part of the twentieth century are not unlike those faced by the Puritans in England in the mid-seventeenth century. Like the English Puritans many American Christians are disillusioned with the great experiment in establishing a godly commonwealth based on biblical principles. The contrast between the idealism of a just society founded on the Bible and the realities of political life as practiced among sinful people is sometimes stark. Like the English Puritans many American evangelicals have been sorely disappointed that the majority ultimately did not choose to follow the godly lead and they, along with many other morally concerned people in the country, have been disenchanted with "godly leadership." The line from Cromwell to Nixon seems to many to be one of betrayal.

The main purpose of this book is to call the attention of those Christians commonly designated as evangelicals to the existence, possibilities and perils of civil religion. The difficulties involved in dealing with such an amorphous group are many. On the other hand, the term as generally understood refers to those individuals who adhere to the historic, orthodox Christian faith. More specifically, evangelicals overwhelmingly subscribe to the following theological irreducible minimum: (1) the Bible as the infallible authority for faith and practice among Christians, (2) the necessity of personal, spiritual regeneration through faith in Jesus Christ, and (3) the idea that Christ must exercise lordship over all of life.[35] It goes without saying that, of all people, those who claim that their highest loyalty is to Christ will want to be aware of the dangers as well as the positive aspects and implications of supporting a civil faith.

The thesis of this work is that all American Christians need to re-evaluate their relationship to civil religion in a critical but constructive fashion as the nation enters its third century of existence. Moreover, succeeding chapters will stress that this reassessment will have far-reaching ramifications for the survival of democracy in the United States and for the future of the free proclamation of the gospel in America and elsewhere. In order for evangelicals in particular to make such an evaluation, it is first necessary to know more about how and why it developed in other places and eras. Therefore, the next chapter will trace its history in the Western world from ancient times to the twentieth century. Perhaps this will enable Americans to determine whether or not they have arrived at the same place in their experience that John Owen and his Puritan followers had in 1652 when they expressed disillusionment with Cromwell and the great crusade to make England a godly commonwealth. Has the summer of evangelical Christian influence in American political life ended? Is the harvest of the fields of biblical values upon which generations of Americans depended for their cultural sustenance over? Has civil religion left the people of God in America morally parched and without spiritual refreshment? Is it too late? Is this a time of the twilight of the saints in America?

2
CIVIL RELIGION FROM THE ANCIENT PAST TO THE ANXIOUS PRESENT

When the distinguished British journalist G. K. Chesterton returned from his first visit to the United States in 1921, he yielded to convention and wrote about his experiences in the New World. As he himself quipped: "Everybody who goes to America for a short time is expected to write a book; and nearly everybody does."[1] Whatever the case, Chesterton's volume has endured, whereas the efforts of less astute observers who wielded duller pens have long since been forgotten. In his essay "What Is America?" Chesterton made the widely cited observation that the United States is "a nation with the soul of a church." Historian Sidney E. Mead picked up the phrase and made it the basis of a well-known essay (with the same title) in which he portrays the religion of the republic as a cosmopolitan faith that serves as the basis of American national unity.[2]

What did Chesterton mean when he declared that America was "a nation with the soul of a church"? As he explained in his essay, the United States was a unique political entity because it was "the only nation in the world . . . founded upon a creed."[3] That creed, he argued, was set forth with dogmatic and even theological lucidity in the Declaration of Independence which he considered to be a first-rate treatise on practical and theoretical politics as well as great literature. He drew a parallel between the Christian church and the American Republic, contending that both had a definite theological notion of what a Christian and an American respectively were. Both drew certain parameters outside of which a Christian (in the case of the church) and an American (in the case of the United States) could not exist. Thus, Christianity and the United States had rather clearly defined theologies, but neither excluded people on the basis of race, nationality or ethnic origin.

Chesterton stressed that the Declaration of Independence made it clear that Americans could be many things, but they could not be anarchists because the document strongly endorsed the concept of government. Nor could they be atheists because it affirmed a virile belief in the Creator. Therefore, although he thought it amusing, he understood why he was asked to respond to the following questions on his visa application for entry into the United States: "Are you an anarchist?" "Are you in favor of subverting the government of the United States by force?" "Are you a polygamist?" He concluded from this:

America invites all men to become citizens; but it implies the dogma that there is such a thing as citizenship. Only, so far as its primary ideal is concerned, its exclusiveness is religious because it is not racial. The missionary can condemn a cannibal, precisely because he cannot condemn a Sandwich Islander. And in something of the same spirit the American may exclude a polygamist, precisely because he cannot exclude a Turk.[4]

In so many words Chesterton was saying that America was a quasi-sacral society with quasi-religious beliefs related in some unspecified way to Christian values. These identifiable beliefs were contained mainly—but not exclusively—in the Declaration of Independence. Most importantly, Chesterton maintained there was a definite American theology with specific dogmas which differentiated Americans from all other peoples and to which those who wanted to become "American" had to subscribe.

A main point of the previous chapter was the fact that as the United States entered its third century it was adrift: socially, politically, morally and spiritually. A bitter irony of the Bicentennial celebration was the obvious absence of consensus on the broad issues of national life. American politics and society in the second half of the twentieth century lack any indication of the presence of what might be called a general will. In short, it is increasingly difficult to determine with any precision what it means to be an American and to ascertain a national purpose and goal. The nation with the soul of a church which Chesterton discovered on his journey to the United States in 1921 apparently no longer exists. What has happened? Is there no longer a religion of the republic? Or has American civil religion become so diluted and so secularized that it no longer is meaningful? And what has happened to the distinctive Christian influence which apparently pervaded the American theology which Chesterton mentioned in his essay? How did America and its civil faith arrive at the place where they stand today?

The answers to these and related questions are obviously too complex to work out in a short discussion of this nature. However, a brief analytical survey of the history of civil religion is necessary for an understanding of American civil religion today. A knowledge of that history will enable evangelical Christians to measure their own faith against the civil one in a more meaningful way and will answer some of the questions heretofore raised and suggest answers to numerous others.[5]

Civil Religion According to Rousseau   Interestingly enough, the thinker who is credited with coining the term *civil religion* did so in a work written fourteen years before the Declaration of Independence. Jean-Jacques Rousseau introduced the phrase in his widely read and influential essay *The Social Contract*, published in 1762. All who study the history of civil religion have to deal with him. Rousseau, of course, no more invented civil religion than Karl Marx invented communism. These two men simply described something which already existed or had existed historically, and each added his own particular interpretation or variation of that phenomenon which he identified. Marx attempted to make socialism scientific while Rousseau struggled to create enlightened civil religion.

Rousseau, a Genevan by birth, was first and foremost a cosmopolitan individual committed to the ideals of the Enlightenment. This eighteenth-century intellectual movement came to be identified closely with his name and those of his fellow philosophes—the French men of letters Voltaire, Diderot, Montesquieu—and the English philosopher John Locke. Rousseau and his associates believed in reason, natural law and progress. They held that human reason could free people of their ills and lead them infallibly to perpetual peace, utopian government and a perfect society. Reason would discover the natural laws regulating existence, thereby insuring the progress of the human race. All of their thought was colored by a belief in the fundamental goodness of human beings and the ability of people to improve themselves by their own efforts.[6]

Rousseau's major contribution to the quest for enlightened government and a better society was his *Social Contract*. It became a kind of secular bible to the people of the Enlightenment, one that outlined a political theory based on the consent of the governed while attempting to reconcile the conflicting demands of individual liberty and social organization. Using Locke's basic assumption concerning a social contract and to some extent his concept of natural law, Rousseau expounded the doctrines of popular sovereignty, the supremacy of the people and the right of revolution. Unfortunately, his effort to harmonize individual freedom with membership in a social group ruled by law is incomplete, often puzzling and open to a variety of interpretations.[7]

These inadequacies aside, much in Rousseau's work found its way into modern constitutional thought. Among other matters he tried to resolve the problem of the relationship between society and religion in an enlightened but pluralistic state. In so doing, he acknowledged that "no state was ever founded without having religion as its basis." But Christianity, the most pervasive faith in the West, was defective because it weakened the state by creating a dual allegiance in its followers. Moreover, it was clear that a Christian's highest loyalty was to God rather than to any political entity even though it was equally evident that Christians could live at peace in a state which allowed them freedom of worship. Civil religion was the device Rousseau hit upon to solve the problem of religious allegiance and dual loyalties. At the same time it would provide a larger moral context against which the behavior of the body politic might be measured in order to restrain any propensity of the political whole to express itself selfishly. But primarily the civic faith would be a means of dealing with socioreligious diversity while cementing people's religious allegiance to civil society. Also, it was a way to achieve and ensure social peace after the disruptive religiously-inspired wars of the sixteenth and seventeenth centuries.

Working from this context, he added a section entitled "Civil Religion" to his *Social Contract* which declared:

There is therefore a purely civil profession of faith of which the Sovereign should fix the articles, not exactly as religious dogmas, but as social sentiments without which a man cannot be a good citizen or a faithful subject. . . . The dogmas of civil religion ought to be few, simple, and exactly worded, without explanation or comment. The existence of a mighty, intelligent, and beneficent Divinity, possessed of foresight and providence, the life to come, the happiness of the just, the punishment of the wicked, the sanctity of the social contract and the laws: these are its positive dogmas.[8]

In short, his civil religion would provide the moral glue for the body politic created by the social contract. Or to put it another way, it would be the general will of the people expressed religiously in the life of the state with a benign but watchful deistic god to preside over the keeping of the public faith.[9]

In many ways Christianity in medieval Europe and religion in general in other societies prior to the eighteenth century served as the social cement which Rousseau envisioned as the main purpose of his enlightened civil faith. However, civil religion in his scheme assumes a much more vital role because the context is more than political. Civil society becomes the focus of the Deity's work on earth, the way to the new heavens and the new earth and the ark of social salvation. It is the center of mankind's religious as well as political loyalty. In this civil society with its civil religion, people find security and freedom, and express themselves morally and rationally. In short, civil religion is the vehicle by which the individual members of Rousseau's body politic find identity and meaning in the life of the state. It becomes the focal point of an individual's civic life while conventional religions (such as Christianity) are relegated to the sphere of private conscience alone.[10]

Further, Rousseau's civil religion appears to have no transcendental reference point. Although it is true that earlier in the *Social Contract* he refers to "the gods" as the only infallible source of true law, still his stress on the contract and the central role of the body politic make it difficult to deny the sovereignty of the general will. Civil faith in a society devoid of the Christian emphasis on a transcendent personal God stands under no higher law. For Rousseau human reason is the key to discerning the general will and, although perhaps not infallible, it certainly assumes all of the attributes of transcendence. In other words, reason enables each individual member of the body politic to read the revelation of God in his creation. Thus, for many practitioners of Rousseau's civil religion before and since, the state encompasses everything that matters, and there is no law or loyalty higher than the state. This also means that in a religiously plural state in which evangelical Christianity is only one of several faiths, it is always in danger of losing its witness to the political institutions if it is co-opted into the larger and more all-encompassing civil faith. The likelihood of idolatrous subservience to the state is always there in Rousseau's overarching civil religion because it has no fixed transcendental reference point by which the nations can and will be judged.[11]

Ancient Civil Religions Did such a civil religion exist in the ancient world of Greece and Rome? Yes, even though Rousseau himself rejected paganism along with the Roman Catholic church and evangelical Christianity as models for his civil religion. He excluded paganism because it was founded on error; Roman Christianity because it divided people's loyalties between two codes of legislation, two rulers, and two countries; and evangelical Christianity because it had no connection to the body politic and failed to bind the hearts of the citizens to the state.[12]

Nevertheless, an examination of Rousseau's criteria suggests that the pagan state religions of Greece and Rome were fairly close to his ideals in most respects, other than being based on what he considered as error. In fact, Émile Durkheim went even further in his study of the role of religion in primitive society and claimed that a common religion is constitutive of the unity and character of every society. He stressed that all societies need some kind of overarching religion with which the vast majority of its people can identify and reaffirm at regular intervals by means of collective ideas and sentiments. Thus, he called attention to the existence in ancient times of what Rousseau and others later would call civil religion—a societal religion sustained by common beliefs and ceremonials.[13]

More specifically, in ancient Greece and Rome the official religion was the handmaiden of the state, gave it moral coherence and served as its social cement in the manner that Rousseau postulated civil religion should. Also, he taught that civil religion should be tolerant of all except those who would not accept the simple dogmas of the public faith or who pretended to accept them and really did not. In Rousseau's ideal state the antisocial ones were to be banished and those guilty of hypocrisy punished by death. Thus, in 399 B.C. Socrates was condemned by an Athenian jury on a charge of introducing strange gods and corrupting the youth of the city-state. Whether or not these were trumped-up accusations against a man who had professed reverence for the laws of Athens is beside the point. There is little doubt that he had tampered with the religio-political order of the day, one which Rousseau later would call civil religion.[14]

Socrates' pupil Plato discussed the order of being and its relation to civil theology in his classic work *The Republic*. Like Rousseau, Plato outlined a minimum body of creedal truths which must be maintained in a viable state. These closely resembled the general beliefs outlined in the *Social Contract*. For example, Plato (like Rousseau) posited belief in a beneficent Deity and argued that among the essential conditions for achieving a just political order was the practice of citizens honoring the gods and their parents. Further, he advocated that all citizens of the state be forced to accept this simple civil religious creed. In short a central element of Plato's civil theology was the need for fundamental consensus through a minimum dogma that lay beyond public debate, and this elementary civic faith would serve as the social glue of the Athenian state.[15]

The Roman Empire provides an even clearer example of the concept of civil religion in ancient times. In the first century A.D. the Roman state became a quasi-religious society, cemented by a common allegiance to the emperor himself. Eventually he was worshiped as a manifest god and savior by his subjects as part of the imperial state cult which served as the civil religion of the realm. Various religions existed alongside it and their adherents could practice their faith as enthusiastically as they pleased as long as they gave nominal acceptance to the state cult, an action which was absolutely obligatory. The position of the emperor in the state cult was a peculiar one since he served as *pontifex maximus* (chief priest) but at the same time increasingly became an object of worship himself.[16]

As the empire drifted from crisis to crisis in the three centuries after Christ, a civil faith that would unify the masses and sanctify the state's claims to authority became a necessity for the Roman rulers. From Decius (249-251) and Diocletian (258-305) to Theodosius the Great (379-395), the emperors tried to strengthen the ideological sanctions supporting the state, mostly through the device of a civil religion. Referring to this situation, the celebrated historian Edward Gibbon noted: "The various modes of worship which prevailed in the Roman world were all considered by the people as equally true; by the philosophers as equally false; and by the magistrates as equally useful."[17]

The early Christians suffered severe persecution because of their stubborn refusal to cooperate with those rulers who sought to establish a viable civil faith by grafting the growing and dynamic Christian faith onto the tree of Roman civil religion. They realized that the Christian God was a jealous God who would brook no rivals, certainly not that of a mere earthly emperor. As a result the Christians refused to sacrifice to Caesar as the state cult required, and thereupon were adjudged enemies of the state, guilty of sedition and treated accordingly.[18]

In their attempts to strengthen and expand civil religion and later when they tried to co-opt Christianity for state purposes, the emperors often were frustrated. Roman imperial civil religion never worked as well as they had hoped. Even Constantine I (312-337) apparently blundered when he thought that he could use Christianity to help sustain the social and political integrity of the empire. Instead, he and his successors learned that the Christians' first allegiance was to the "City of God" rather than to the "City of Man." Gibbon may have been wrong in pointing to Christianity as a main reason for the fall of the Roman Empire, but if the Christian community did not bring about Rome's political disintegration, neither did it provide substantial and necessary support for the tottering state. Eventually Rome staggered off into historical oblivion while the Christian faith remained to form the basis of a new civilization.[19]

In the course of its struggle with the Roman state and subsequent emergence as the majority faith of the empire, Christianity lost something. To some extent its position vis-à-vis the world was compromised, and Christians accepted the imperial idea of a universal society based upon quasi-religious assumptions. Unity was understood to be organizational, and an unfortunate liaison was established between the City of God and the City of Man which bore tasteless if not bitter fruit during the Middle Ages.[20]

Medieval and Renaissance Civil Religion: Eclipse and Resurgence The Christian commonwealth which emerged during the last years of the Roman Empire dominated Western culture for nearly a thousand years. It is difficult to find viable civil religion in the Middle Ages until late in the period. The Western mind in the feudal age was reluctant to accept the ancient Roman and Greek emphases on civic virtues in connection with a civil religion, and the very nature of the feudal system militated against this. Moreover, the concept of fatherland, so common in the ancient world, had lost its religious flavor and connotations, and Christians increasingly were called upon to choose between pope and king in terms of ultimate loyalties. The story of medieval church-state relations is too complex to rehearse here, but it will suffice to note that the struggle between church and state for religious and political supremacy consumed the energies of the popes and feudal princes. Not until the twelfth and thirteenth centuries was there a hint of a return to a concept of civil religion in terms of a cosmopolitan, state-oriented common faith.

In an absorbing study entitled "*Pro Patria Mori* in Medieval Thought" published in 1951, Ernst H. Kantorowicz commented at length on the emergence of civil religion in Western Europe in the late Middle Ages, even though that was not the primary focus of his essay. Long before the recent surge of interest in the topic, he dealt with themes closely related to civil religion in an examination of the place of the concept of "death for the fatherland" in late medieval political and religious thought. His conclusion was that something closely resembling modern-day civil religion had begun to develop in this period.[21]

During most of the Middle Ages the patria of the Christians was not any earthly fatherland but heaven, the celestial city of the blessed. However, with the emergence of national monarchies in the twelfth and thirteenth centuries, a gradual shift from heaven back to earth, so to speak, began as the patria came to refer to a national kingdom or to the crown as the visible symbol of a national territorial community. Devices that facilitated this shift included taxation for the defense of the realm (which eventually became the patria), the politicizing of the Crusades (more taxation: what was good for the realm of Christ in the Holy Land was good for those of France and England respectively), the transfer of the concept of the holy soil overseas to the holy soil of the French or English fatherland, the association of the martyrdom of people slain on a crusade with that for the earthly fatherland, and the common habit of sanctifying any defense of the realm with the slogan "for God and crown!"[22]

Most important of all for the history of civil religion was the emergence of the organic concept of the state. According to this mode of thinking, which developed out of the experiences of the Crusades and the wars of the period, the king was the head and his subjects the members of the body politic. Reason and nature demanded that all members of the body serve the head as well as be controlled by it. Moreover, the king's peace was not only that of the realm but also of the church, of learning, virtue and justice, and it permitted the concentration of forces for the reconquest of the Holy Land. Soon war for France was equated with war for the Holy Land. It was in this context that Joan of Arc cried: "Those who wage war against the holy realm of France, wage war against King Jesus!"[23] This remarkable fifteenth-century French peasant girl articulated a concept shared in common with her better educated contemporaries—the French were a peculiar people chosen by the Lord to carry out the orders of heaven.

This adduction of the organic concept of the state is tied in with another major change in late medieval political and religious thought. Originally referring to the Eucharist, the term *corpus mysticum* after 1150 (following the great debate over the nature of the Eucharist as a sacrament) was gradually transferred to the church as an organized body in order to reinforce the concept of unity there. Pope Boniface VIII in his bull *Unam Sanctam* (1302) proclaimed as official doctrine that the church was "one mystical body the head of which is Christ." This use of the term *corpus mysticum* to designate the church in its sociological and ecclesiological aspects was adopted at a critical moment in church history.[24]

The new use of the term *corpus mysticum* linked the rapidly growing ecclesiastical organization of the church with the former liturgical sphere, but at the same time it placed the church as a political organism on a level with the secular bodies politic which by that time were starting to assert themselves as self-sufficient communities. Moreover, in an age of secularizing tendencies this terminological change coincided with that period in the history of Western thought when corporative and organic doctrines began to pervade political thinking. Political communities, large and small, borrowed from the church and applied the term *corpus mysticum* to themselves, using it for their own justification and their own ends. During the fourteenth century the term came to mean any *corpus morale et politicum* (political and moral body), church or state. Thus, every person was regarded as belonging to some "mystical body," some social collective or aggregate. Some interpreted this as Holy Mother Church, others as mankind, but still others as patria, the fatherland.

The upshot of this was that more and more Europeans thought of themselves as citizens of a state in religious and moral terms. As the national monarchies increased in size and strength they utilized every means at their disposal to secure the loyalty of their subjects. In the fourteenth and fifteenth centuries when pope and king frequently clashed, Christian people in Western Europe often gave fundamental allegiance to their monarch, for whatever reason, but with an increasingly state-oriented and state-initiated religious sanction. Eventually the state sloughed off from the church and appropriated for itself ethical values and moral emotions which were essentially absent in the earlier Middle Ages but had dominated civil religion in antiquity.

Kantorowicz shows how the politicized idea of the *corpus mysticum* received wide acceptance among the humanists of Renaissance Italy in the fifteenth century. The growth of the city-states in Italy and the nation-states elsewhere in Europe was accompanied by a resurgence of a viable civil piety. In its new version the older medieval theme was shifted from the "mystical body of the church the head of which is Christ" to the newer emphasis on "the mystical body of the state the head of which is the prince." Kantorowicz concluded:

> Here the parallelism of spiritual *corpus mysticum* and secular *corpus mysticum*, of the mystical body's divine head and its princely head, of self-sacrifice for the heavenly transcendental community and self-sacrifice for the terrestrial metaphysical community has reached a certain point of culmination. And from this high-point onward the historian will find it easy to coast down that road which ultimately leads to early modern, modern, and ultra-modern statisms.[25]

The sixteenth century marked the end of the medieval synthesis and the beginning of cultural and religious pluralism in the West. It was a time of religious turmoil and change brought about by the Protestant, Catholic and Radical Reformations. Renaissance intellectual developments, the rise of the nation-states, the exploration and exploitation of the New World, and raging inflation helped make the sixteenth one of the most tumultuous of all centuries. The great age of revolutions and civil wars had begun. The future lay with those states which could create a secular base for the maintenance of public peace. In the late seventeenth and early eighteenth centuries as the so-called wars of religion subsided and the new national states stabilized, civil religion reappeared all over Europe. It developed most fully in countries where "enlightened despots" nursed civil faith after the Rousseau model.[26]

Civil Religion in Modern Europe   The exact character of civil religion in Europe during the past two centuries is not altogether clear, and much research remains to be done in this area. Existing studies of civil religion and related topics of the period are largely inconclusive. Clear distinctions are not always made between civil religion and particularistic state churches. The pluralistic element which fostered the construction of a civil religion may have been secularism (or perhaps secular humanism) rather than a rival religion that sought to challenge established churches. State churches undoubtedly served the purposes of civil religion in some instances, especially in multiethnic countries. Further, nationalism in many countries took on features of religion, including the claim to ultimate and universal reality, but nationalism is not by itself civil religion. To be sure, both secularism and nationalism substituted earthly, utilitarian values and ends for transcendent ones. Historian Ronald VanderMolen, for example, concludes that neither biblical Christianity nor anything like modern American civil religion is a major configuration on the religious and political contours of post-Napoleonic Europe, and what actually exists are secularized societies which contain a residue of genuine Christian ideals and values.[27]

On the other hand a recent study of civil faith in Nazi Germany by David J. Diephouse provides evidence of a recognizable civil religion there. As Professor Diephouse points out:

> For the Nazi true believer, Hitler's order inspired loyalty
> through its apocalyptic political gospel and the charis-

matic personal appeal of the Führer. For a much broader range of Germans, however, the regime's legitimacy rested upon its ability to exploit the troubled reservoir of historic German attitudes towards the state and nation.[28] This scholar suggests that Hitler's Germany had a public faith that was at once a folk religion, the transcendent universal religion of the nation and religious nationalism. But, he hastens to add that it also was more than this. The Third Reich was a "synthetic barbarism," as Reinhold Niebuhr once put it, in which the state became fused with an explicit religion of the state. Jacques Ellul suggests that the real essence of Nazi Germany was secularism come full circle. Perhaps the Hitler regime is a valid example of civil religion carried to its logical conclusion; that is, it ultimately led to the disappearance of all conventional distinctions between the sacred and the secular, and religious fervor was effectively transferred from the realm of faith to that of politics. Moreover, Nazi civil religion had no transcendental reference point other than the state itself. Hitler may have fulfilled Rousseau's ideal of civil religion better than he knew.[29]

Anglo-American Civil Religion Civil religion in an advanced form developed in sixteenth and seventeenth-century England under the aegis of the Church of England. Although the Anglican establishment was technically a state church and not civil religion, within it was such diversity and latitude that it can be considered a form of civil faith. Certainly after the death of Elizabeth I in 1603, there was a conscious need for an overarching civil religion as the sectarians multiplied and began to express themselves denominationally.

The relatively early development of civil religion in modern England is important for American religious history as well. Even as the majority of the basic political and social ideas which molded America originated in the British Isles, so did most of the concepts of the New World brand of civil religion. American civil piety grew out of a fusion of elements of Enlightenment and Puritan thought, ideas which crossed the Atlantic mainly from England.

The most noticeable ingredient of the nascent English civil religion of the later sixteenth century was the feeling that England was God's "New Israel" and the English were his "covenanted people." This conviction was expressed as early as 1559 by Bishop John Aylmer who asserted that "God is English," and put these words into the mouth of England who spoke to her beloved subjects: "Besides this, God hath brought forth in me the greatest and excellentest treasure that he hath for your comfort and all the world's. He would that out of my womb should come that servant of his, your brother John Wyclif, who begat Luther, who begat truth."[30]

John Foxe popularized the "chosen nation" theme in his incredibly influential *Book of Martyrs*, first published in 1563. In this and many later printings Foxe outlined the classic providential tale of England's unique role in history. The great cosmic struggle between God and Satan underlay all of human history with England serving as God's chosen instrument of victory. God led the English nation steadfastly forward to its rendezvous with destiny, according to Foxe. From Wyclif to Henry VIII and his break with Rome to the first Elizabeth, England was guided by God's hand in defying the antichrist, that is, the papacy. The day would come when England would fulfill its divine destiny, free the world from papal bondage and usher in the millennium. The specific way he would accomplish his plan was not always clear during the stormy period from 1563 to 1642, but one thing was certain: England was God's anointed vessel![31]

As it turned out Parliament was the instrument God would use to carry out his sacred purposes; or at least that was the dominant view in 1641 when Foxe's *Book of Martyrs* underwent its eighth printing and the country teetered on the brink of civil war. English people in general, but especially the Puritans, likened themselves and their nation to ancient Israel. However, just as God's covenant with the Jewish people was conditional, so too was his covenant with England. They were not only a chosen people but also a covenant people standing under God's judgment and ultimately accountable to him.[32]

These impressions of England's special relation to God were strengthened during the English Civil War and the Commonwealth period (1642-1658) under the leadership of Oliver Cromwell. But the Puritan understanding of England's covenant status was modified during the 1650s when that country developed a full-blown civil religion with its great emphasis on transcendence. In this period the Puritans, especially Cromwell, rejected the view that an elect state was not bound by the normal canons of civic morality and adopted a stance linking politics, morality and religion, which allowed Christian truth to transcend and control the world of politics.

On the other hand, there is evidence that points to a gap between theory and practice in the English Puritan Commonwealth. Although the Puritans made a theoretical distinction between the state as God's chosen agent of salvation and the state as the protector of societal stability, apparently in practice they did not always observe this distinction. In short, English civil religion was a mixed bag. Many of the events of the Cromwell years contradicted the stated ideals of the Commonwealth, such as the separation of church and state. There was also an ominous tendency to substitute the state for the church and to substitute peace, freedom and material prosperity for the gospel's emphasis on the world of the spirit.[33]

These were some of the reasons that Dr. John Owen and other seventeenth-century English evangelicals became disenchanted with the great Puritan republican experiment. "They had looked for other things from them that professed Christ," wrote Owen. Little wonder that they felt that the summer had slipped by and the harvest was over and still they were not refreshed.[34] Although Cromwell and the Puritans ultimately failed in their effort to complete the Reformation and establish their envisioned semisectarian state church, the imagery of England as a chosen vessel lingered long after their demise.

A portion of the Puritan ethos and world view was assimilated by John Locke and funneled into the Enlightenment. For example, much of what Locke had to say about civil theology appealed to both common sense and revelation as contained in the Holy Scriptures. He picked up and broadened the Puritan ideal of limited toleration within the framework of a required minimum body of civil and religious dogma, and he added to the Puritan world view a certain rationality based on natural law and reason. Much of this later found its way into the thinking of Rousseau.[35]

But more important, the Puritans carried their notion of an elect nation—the New Israel, a city upon a hill—with them to America, and they came with a strong sense of transcendent responsibility to the God of the universe. The Pilgrims and Puritans of Massachusetts, the Quakers of Pennsylvania, the Baptists of Rhode Island, the Anglicans of Virginia and the Presbyterian and Reformed churches of New Jersey gave America its first identity. Although they possessed an essentially evangelical Christian world view, they did not arrive with a fully-developed civil faith to fit the American situation. That would come from their experience in America itself.

Understanding American Civil Religion   There are at least five components in the formulation of the initial American civil religion. The *first* was the *chosen nation theme* brought by the Puritans from the mother country. It provided a theological foundation for a theological people and a degree of self-awareness seldom equaled in other political societies before or after. From this base flowed the central core of beliefs which made the United States what Chesterton called "a nation with the soul of a church." Because this point is absolutely fundamental, it requires fuller attention.

The early Americans, especially those who settled in New

England, knew who they were and what they wanted to do. In this respect the Pilgrims of Plymouth occupied a special place in the hearts and minds of those who lived in the colonies, and Sam Adams and others of "the boys" during the Revolutionary War period often referred to "Mother Plymouth." The Mayflower Compact manifested that the Pilgrims envisioned the establishment of a godly, moral and just society based on biblical principles. This was true even though the Mayflower carried passengers who were both "saints and strangers," as William Bradford, the first governor of Plymouth Plantation, described the religious mix of the 1620 Massachusetts settlement.[36]

When this resolute little band of Separatists (nonconforming English Protestants) sighted the Cape Cod coast of Massachusetts, they realized that they were far north of the site to which they had been granted patent privileges by the Virginia Company. The absence of valid rights to the Plymouth area caused considerable uneasiness among those on board the Mayflower, especially the non-Separatists. In an effort to hold the group together the Pilgrim leaders persuaded forty-one male passengers to sign a solemn pledge known as the Mayflower Compact. The famous Compact became not only the constitution of the new colony but also a foundational statement of American civil religion and one of the most revered documents among those modern American evangelicals who cherish the notion that the United States is a Christian nation. More than any other piece of literature in early American history, it provided the ideological cornerstone for a period which might be described as "the morning of the saints."

The Compact stated that the purpose of the Plymouth colony was to establish a "civil body politic" which would honor God and advance the Christian faith:

In the name of God, amen. We whose names are underwritten, the loyal subjects of our dread sovereign lord, King James, by the grace of God, of Great Britain, France, and Ireland King, Defender of the Faith, etc., having undertaken, for the glory of God, and advancement of the Christian faith, and honor of our King and country, a voyage to plant the first colony in the northern parts of Virginia, do by these presents solemnly and mutually, in the presence of God and one another, covenant and combine ourselves together into a civil body politic, for our better ordering and preservation and furtherance of the ends aforesaid; and equal laws, ordinances, acts, constitutions, and offices, from time to time, as shall be thought most meet and convenient for the general good of the colony, unto which we promise all due submission and obedience.[37]

This document and Governor Bradford's history of the early years of the colony reflect a theological awareness and a sense of identity and destiny which was to set the tone for the future of New England and in many ways for America itself.[38]

But even more than the Pilgrims, the Puritans who settled in Massachusetts north of Plymouth beginning in 1630 brought with them a unique theological-political concept which has helped mold the American psyche from that day to the present; namely, that the Puritan settlers of New England were God's chosen people. The Cambridge-educated lawyer John Winthrop, a person described by contemporaries as modest, tender, self-sacrificing and devoutly Christian, was the most distinguished governor of Massachusetts Bay Colony. It was Winthrop who endowed America with the imagery of the "city upon a hill."

While in midocean on the *Arbella* Winthrop composed his single most important political statement, "A Modell of Christian Charity." This tract endeavored to show the unity of the civil state that the shipload of Puritans hoped to found in Massachusetts. It was to guide the passengers when they set up their business corporation in the New World (the Massachusetts Bay Company) and to aid them in constituting a polity.

Winthrop applied a theory of the organic community to the new enterprise, stressed the special covenant relationship which those who knew God through Jesus Christ enjoyed, and pointed out that God expected unique behavior from his people. Only when the people of the Massachusetts Bay Colony realized that God had covenanted with the community and that the welfare of each person depended on the welfare of the body politic, would the members comprehend the love of neighbor which was to be the cohesive element of the corporation. If only the Puritans of the new colony would really covenant with each other to form a polity based on true godliness and biblical principles, then they would enjoy peace and plenty. In language that became immortal in American history Winthrop explained that as a result of a genuine social covenant based on the Bible:

> ... wee shall finde that the God of Israell is among us, when tenn of us shall be able to resist a thousand of our enemies, when hee shall make us a prayse and glory, that men shall say of succeeding plantacions: the lord make it like that of New England: for wee must Consider that wee shall be a Citty upon a Hill, the eies of all people are uppon us.[39]

Thus, according to Winthrop, he and his associates were involved in a mission of tremendous significance. They were the test case which would determine whether people could live on earth according to the will of God. Whereas the Puritans were being frustrated in their attempt to bring the Reformation to a logical and successful conclusion in England, they now had the opportunity to do so in New England. If they succeeded, their outpost in the wilderness would be as a "city upon a hill," a moral and political example to the entire world. Their Zion would be the hub of the universe whose light and wisdom would radiate in all directions for the good of mankind and the glory of God! This belief became a part of the ideology of Puritan New England and eventually of the majority of Americans in the eighteenth and nineteenth centuries.

Moreover, the Pilgrims, Puritans, Quakers, Baptists, Anglicans, Presbyterians and Reformed congregations of colonial America possessed a political outlook which contained a strong sense of transcendent responsibility to the God of the universe, and their theological stance was one which twentieth-century evangelical Christians would generally find congenial. These religious refugees, even more than those who came to the British colonies for other reasons, gave America its first and most lasting identity.

The chosen people theme coalesced with the American Revolution. The success of the colonies in throwing off British rule confirmed the uniqueness of the American experience and laid the foundation for an elaborate civil theology. The propensity of the Founding Fathers to see the Revolution as a plateau in the development of America is illustrated by the manner in which John Adams and many of his contemporaries repeatedly reminded the younger generation that the "real revolution" had been accomplished in American hearts long before 1776.[40]

More than any other single identifiable religious group, the Puritans and other Calvinists infused early American thought with the goal of transforming society and creating a new kind of people, theologically and politically. Although the majority of Americans in the seventeenth and eighteenth centuries—including many evangelicals—were not Puritans in any strict doctrinal sense, Puritan values and the ideal of the New Israel still permeated almost every aspect of American political thought. Fused with rational elements from deism (to be discussed later in this chapter), the doctrines, themes and ceremonies of a distinctively American civil religion began to emerge.

The Declaration of Independence, the Constitution and later Abraham Lincoln's Gettysburg Address became the sacred scriptures of the new public faith. As historians John E. Smylie, Conrad Cherry and others have noted, early colonial Christians believed that their own church covenants were vehicles of God's participation in history. However, the Declaration of Independence and the Constitution eventually became the covenants which bound the people of the nation together in a political-religious union and secured for them God's blessing, protection and summons to historic mission. Chesterton, then, was at least partially correct in commenting that the creed of the American nation was the Declaration of Independence.[41]

The growth of American civil religion also entailed the development of leadership imagery and heroic founding figures parallel to those contained in the biblical account of the chosen nation of Israel, thus leading to the Founding Fathers mythology. Based partly on fact and partly on need, the revolutionary leaders Benjamin Franklin, George Washington, John Adams and Thomas Jefferson were lionized. Over the years Washington became the Moses figure, Jefferson the prophet and Lincoln the theologian of the national faith.

Especially intriguing is the historical evolution of Washington as a symbol of civil faith—a veritable mirror reflecting the beliefs of countless generations of Americans. Almost immediately following his death in 1799, the first president was eulogized as an American Moses. The noted Boston preacher Thaddeus Fiske in a service commemorating Washington's passing expressed an already widely-held idea when he intoned: "As the deliverer and political savior of our nation, he has been the same to us, as Moses was to the Children of Israel."[42] The imagery was almost irresistible. Probably no analogy has been so well articulated as the view that Washington truly had been a Moses for America, the man who led his people from tyranny to freedom. Thus, in keeping with the self-picture of the Americans as the new covenant people of God, their veneration of the American Moses persisted as a vital element of their belief in the providential guidance of the country well into the twentieth century.

Eventually something of this sacred-leader, father-figure role was transferred to each of the presidents. The words and acts of the Founding Fathers, especially the first few presidents, shaped the form and tone of American civil religion.

In their presidential pronouncements the early chief executives reinforced and expounded upon the chosen nation theme. Jefferson in his Second Inaugural Address on March 4, 1805, tied together a chosen people and their leaders:

I shall need, too, the favor of that Being in whose hands we are, who led our fathers, as Israel of old, from their native land and planted them in a country flowing with all the necessaries and comforts of life; who has covered our infancy with His providence and our riper years with His wisdom and power, and to whose goodness I ask you to join in supplications with me that He will so enlighten the minds of your servants, guide their councils, and prosper their measures that whatsoever they do shall result in your good, and shall secure to you the peace, friendship, and approbation of all nations.[43]

The imagery is complete: Europe is Egypt, America the promised land and God has led his people to establish a new social order which will be a "city upon a hill."[44]

During the first hundred years of nationhood American civil religion developed its own set of political-religious ceremonies and symbols. These rites, holidays and symbols fused patriotism with piety and, to some extent, melded God and country. To illustrate, many scholars refer to Memorial Day as the great holiday and holy day of American civil religion. As Conrad Cherry notes:

The Memorial Day celebration is an American sacred ceremony, a religious ritual, a modern cult of the dead. Although it shares the theme of redemptive sacrifice with Christianity and other religions, and although the devotees would insist that the God invoked is the God of Judaism and Christianity, the Memorial Day rite is a national service that unites Protestants, Catholics and Jews beyond their differences.[45]

In fact the same generalization holds for Thanksgiving Day and the Fourth of July. The ritual and language used to celebrate these special national days is not that of any particular denomination or even of a broadly defined evangelical

Christianity, but of a larger national faith which permits the participants to unite with their fellows to confront mutual enemies and to satisfy the need for a common identity and sense of destiny. In the case of Memorial Day the sentiment of a threefold unity is dramatically expressed—a unity of the living among themselves, of all the living to all the dead, and of all the living and dead as a group to the Deity.

As Memorial Day serves to integrate the local community into the civil religion, so Thanksgiving Day ties in the family. Moreover, the Fourth of July is a time to eulogize the faith of the Founding Fathers and to celebrate the events connected with the establishment of the chosen nation described by Jefferson in his Second Inaugural. Memorial Day, Thanksgiving and Independence Day provide occasions for fusing piety and patriotism and for expressing the belief that the United States has the providential assignment to act as the guardian and promoter of freedom and democracy throughout the world. These holidays, along with minor ones like Veterans Day and perhaps the birthdays of Washington and Lincoln, serve as an annual ritual calendar for American civil religion. And, the public schools—before the mid-twentieth century at least—provided a scene for the cultic celebration of most of the civil rituals.[46]

Other expressions of the overarching faith of the republic include singing "God Bless America" in church and the inclusion of patriotic songs in hymnbooks. It can be detected in the God-talk in the speeches and public remarks of the politicians. It is exemplified by repeated acts of religiosity on the part of recent American presidents.

One final component of the chosen nation motif was added during the Civil War—the introduction of the themes of death, sacrifice and rebirth into the American experience and the ideology of the civil religion. This was symbolized by the life and death of Abraham Lincoln and is expressed vividly in the martyred president's Gettysburg Address. In the same vein the Lincoln Memorial in Washington has become a sacred national temple before which many more recent ceremonies of civil religion have been performed.[47]

The connection between the themes of sacrifice and political piety are clearly illustrated in the prominence assumed by the flag in the symbolism of the American civil religion. Foreign observers frequently have called attention to how America gives a much larger role to its flag than do most other nations. This originated partly in response to the needs of a young nation searching for unifying traditions and symbols, but the flag soon became a virtual end in itself and drew forth from the American people a form of religious devotion. This linkage of religious themes and sentiments and reverence for the flag culminated in the Civil War period when the national banner became a rallying point for all truly patriotic Americans. It was in 1865 that Oliver Wendell Holmes penned the words of a poem entitled "God Save the Flag!" This bit of verse, often cited by civil religionists on the Fourth of July, illustrates vividly how the biblical concepts of sacrifice and the shedding of blood for redemptive purposes could be tied together with loyalty to the nation and its ideals. In Holmes's own richly suggestive words:

Washed in the blood of the brave and the blooming,
Snatched from the altars of insolent foes,
Burning with star-fires, but never consuming,
Flash its broad ribbons of lily and rose.

Vainly the prophets of Baal would rend it,
Vainly his worshippers pray for its fall;
Thousands have died for it, millions defend it,
Emblem of justice and mercy to all. . . .

Borne on the deluge of old usurpations,
Drifting our Ark o'er the desolate seas,
Bearing the rainbow of hope to the nations,
Torn from the storm-cloud and flung to the breeze!

God bless the Flag and its loyal defenders,
While its broad folds o'er the battle-field wave,
Till the dim star-wreath rekindle its splendors,
Washed from its stains in the blood of the brave![48]

Civil Millennialism   Closely related to the chosen nation theme is the *second* factor in the formulation of American civil religion, namely, the *transformation of the "God's New Israel" concept into civil millennialism.* This was already alluded to in discussing the chosen nation motif since national purpose is part and parcel of why Americans saw themselves as an elect people. In other words, Holmes was referring to millennial expectations when he spoke of America as "bearing the rainbow of hope to the nations."

The conversion of the original theistically-oriented chosen nation theme into civil millennialism occurred in the period between the First Great Awakening in the 1730s and 1740s and the outbreak of the Revolution in 1775. Disappointed that the great revival did not result in the dawning of the millennium, many colonial preachers turned their apocalyptic expectations elsewhere. In short when the First Awakening tailed off, its evangelical spokesmen had to reinterpret the millennial hope it had spawned. In the process the clergy, in a subtle but profound shift in religious values, redefined the ultimate goal of apocalyptic hope. The old expectations of the conversion of all nations to Christianity became diluted with, and often subordinated to, the commitment to America as the new seat of liberty. First France and then England became the archenemies of liberty, both civil and religious. In an insightful study of this development, historian Nathan Hatch concludes:

> The civil millennialism of the Revolutionary era, expressed by rationalists as well as pietists, grew directly out of the politicizing of Puritan millennial history in the two decades before the Stamp Act crisis. . . . Civil millennialism advanced freedom as the cause of God, defined the primary enemy as the antichrist of civil oppression rather than that of formal religion, traced the myths of its past through political developments rather than through the vital religion of the forefathers, and turned its vision toward the privileges of Britons rather than to a heritage exclusive to New England.[49]

Thus, the First Great Awakening was not only a tumultuous religious event but also a popular movement with wide-ranging political and ideological implications that laid the groundwork for an emotional and future-oriented American civil religion. The revolutionary generation began to build an American nation based upon the religious foundations of evangelical revivalism. The latter-day New England Puritans were joined by many Anglicans, Presbyterians and Dutch Reformed of equally evangelical persuasion in seeing themselves as jointly commissioned to awaken and guide the nation into the coming period of millennial fulfillment. Most important, Calvinist ideology manifested an astounding capacity for undergoing secularization without losing its moral force.

But in the process, where the churches moved out the nation moved in. As Professor Smylie astutely observes in his study of the role of the churches in the rise of national consciousness:

> Gradually in America the nation emerged as the primary agent of God's meaningful activity in history. Hence Americans bestowed on it a catholicity of destiny similar to that which theology attributes to the universal church.[50]

As mentioned before, most colonial evangelicals believed that their own church covenants were vehicles of God's action in history. However, eventually the Declaration of Independence, the Constitution and the Bill of Rights became the covenants that bound together the people of the nation and secured to them God's blessing, protection and call to historic mission.

In the nineteenth century this secularization of the millennial ideal resulted in what historians generally call Manifest Destiny. This fateful linkage of religious and political sentiments was illustrated by journalist John L. O'Sullivan in the first recorded usage of the term in 1845: "Our manifest destiny [is] to overspread and possess the whole of the continent which Providence has given us for the development of the great experiment of liberty and federative self government entrusted to us."[51] For countless Americans this term came to mean that Almighty God had manifestly destined them to spread over the entire North American continent. And as they did, they would take with them their uplifting and ennobling democratic and religious institutions.

Most Protestants in America embraced this outlook, and they regarded their country as a "redeemer nation" which had a messianic mission to save the world by creating a new humanity based on evangelical religion and democratic institutions. In an 1861 address to the Indiana Methodist Conference, Bishop Matthew Simpson articulated this point of view in its most blatant form:

> God has given us a peculiar position before the nations of the earth.... A nation that has in itself the power to elevate its own citizens, and to exert good influence upon nations abroad, has the especial favor of God.... It is certainly not in God's plan that we should pass away. Then how could the world do without us? The people of all nations look to us. If our country goes down, one-half of the world would raise a wail of woe, and sink lower. God ... cannot afford to lose the United States.[52]

Thus, a secularized evangelical millennialism became the basis of a national messianic sense of destiny. Evangelical and democratic elements were fused into a civil millennialism which became a part of the civil religion of the land.

A Religious Consensus A *third* element in constructing the first American civil religion was some sort of *religious consensus*. Broadly speaking, this was provided by the evangelicals. It came initially with the First Great Awakening which instilled evangelical values, if not theology, firmly in the common people of the young nation. However, Americans at the time of the Revolution were not particularly religious in the conventional sense and in fact formal church membership declined sharply. But with the Second Great Awakening, the revivalists triumphed and gave the nineteenth-century United States its basically evangelical cast. As William G. McLoughlin affirms:

> The story of American Evangelicalism is the story of America itself in the years 1800 to 1900, for it was Evangelical religion which made Americans the most religious people in the world, molded them into a unified, pietistic-perfectionist nation, and spurred them on to those heights of social reform, missionary endeavor, and imperialistic expansionism which constitute the moving forces of our history in that century.[53]

Of course, this was not the civil religion which Rousseau had in mind, but evangelical Christianity did provide the religious glue for the new republic throughout most of the century, thereby meeting Rousseau's requirement for social cohesion. Evangelical Christianity established the ethical norms that transcended parties, sects and creeds as it informed the consciences and molded the lifestyles of three generations of Americans.

At this juncture it is important to emphasize that civil religion is not merely a form of nationalism. Modern nationalism is a state of mind in which an individual assumes that his highest loyalty is due to his nationality and thus all other allegiances are inferior or secondary. It really goes beyond patriotism, that is, it is more than loyalty or love for a certain area, region or country. Nationalism demands that the members of a nation give their highest allegiance to their nation-state or work to create one if this does not already exist.[54] Civil religion is more powerful and profound than nationalism in that it brings together elements of both nationalism and religious commitment. In the American context this resulted in the apparently happy marriage of evangelical Christianity with liberal democracy. Nineteenth-century American Christians felt they could give their whole-hearted political allegiance to the nation because it was God's chosen instrument to spread both Christianity and democracy to all the world. The two concepts were to them as branches of the same evangelical tree. There was no conflict in loyalty to God and loyalty to his chosen nation.

Several scholars have noted this fusion of evangelical and national interests and world views in the nineteenth-century United States. For example, Ralph H. Gabriel in his classic study, *The Course of American Democratic Thought*, underscored the confluence of evangelical Protestantism and democratic ideology in the formulation of what he called the "American Democratic Faith." Pietists, Calvinists and Dissenters all contributed to the evangelical religion of the land which flowed in the same channel as romantic democracy. The parallels between the doctrines of the democratic faith and the fundamental beliefs of evangelical Christianity were remarkable: common assent to a basic moral law, agreement with the Calvinist insistence that constitutional government was necessary for the restraint of evil, the shared doctrine of the free individual, common adherence to the philosophy of progress and accord in the conviction that the mission of America was to save the world from autocracy on the one hand and satanic governance on the other.[55]

This interpenetration of evangelical Christianity and democratic ideals was forcefully illustrated by the universally used *McGuffey's Eclectic Readers*. William H. McGuffey, a college professor and part-time Presbyterian preacher, deliberately attempted to "shape the rising generation to our model." To accomplish this he developed a civil catechism which sold an estimated 120 million copies between 1836 and 1920. The books were designed not only to teach children how to read but also to inculcate in them the American civil faith.[56]

The McGuffey Readers were concerned with the three essential elements in the life of a public; the common story of the people of the nation, a vehicle by which the public can celebrate its history and future by a set of symbolic acts, and ethical directives regarding its common work and destiny. In fulfilling the first essential, the early Puritans were held up as the fathers of the civil faith and the moral heroes of the republic. As for the second, the speaker's platform—solidly embedded in the traditions of the orator and the revivalist—was the chosen vehicle. In the third, the values of evangelical Christianity were portrayed as those of the people, namely, individual responsibility and rectitude, sound literary tastes (based, of course, upon the Bible) and the glorification of hard work and success. The three flowed together to reinforce the conviction that America was God's New Israel and the hope of the world. These evangelical values and their secularized counterparts were acceptable in the main to evangelicals and nonevangelicals alike in the nineteenth-century United States.

Evangelical Values and Deism This leads to the *fourth* component in the making of the first American civil religion —*the intellectual and political elite held social ideals compatible with the prevailing religious temper of the nation.* This amounted to a fusion of the evangelical Christian values of the masses with the deism and near-deism of many of the Founding Fathers and nineteenth-century political leaders. Since the basic faith was evangelical Christianity and the fundamental political viewpoint was democratic, and the two had been largely merged in popular evangelical thought, nearly every intellectual or politician could identify with one or both. Even deists like Franklin, John Adams and Jefferson could join with their fellow Americans in a common front because their basic values were in harmony. As studies of the thought of the American deists attest, the Enlightenment in America was more flexible in its attitude toward organized religion than was its European counterpart, because there was no established church upheld by or upholding a monarchy. Even if the American deists did not enter into the fullness of the evangelical faith, they could imbibe a large portion of its political expression.[57]

A long-standing historical debate rages over whether the liberal democrats influenced the evangelicals more than the evangelicals influenced the liberal democrats, and vice versa, in the formulation of the early American civil religion.

It appears that the two streams—evangelical Christianity with its heavy Puritan component and deism—were twin tributaries which flowed together to form the civil faith of the fledgling American republic. However, in the nineteenth century the evangelicals—especially the Dissenters of the colonial period—gained the upper hand and the deistic element faded into the shadow from whence it would be summoned in the more secular twentieth century.

Gabriel, Mead, Ahlstrom and others have pointed out how this cluster of evangelical-deistic ideals made up the early national faith. As incredible as that may seem, America became the common meeting ground of evangelical Christianity and the Enlightenment, but then the new American republic was an incredible place! For Christians the moral law was the will of God, while for the intellectuals in the Enlightenment tradition it was the natural law of the eighteenth-century philosophes. The central theme of evangelical Christianity was that true liberty comes to the person who has been released by Christ from the fetters of sin. The central theme of the democratic faith was the doctrine of the free individual. Freedom was a common value which was shared by evangelicals and nonevangelicals alike in the early republic. Nineteenth-century American civil religion was based on the interlocking piety of two devoutly held ideologies— deistic politics and evangelical faith—and it rested on a heartfelt belief in the twin concepts of freedom and democracy in the context of a New Israel with a sense of divine mission.[58]

Historical Authentication   *Fifth* and finally, there had to be a *measure of self-authenticating history in the American experience upon which to build a convincing civil religion.* In other words the course of human events had to seem to bear out the fact that the United States was indeed God's chosen nation and that it was ordained to spread civil and religious liberty to the farther regions. The nation, after all, did come into existence and expand by an unprecedented series of events which gave the Union fundamentally transcendent properties which theories of social compact could only partially explain.

Sober rationalists like Jefferson and others of his generation recognized the transcendent quality in the birth of the nation. Jefferson in particular grasped this element and became the prophet of American civil religion: "With a firm reliance on the protection of Divine Providence, we mutually pledge to each other our lives, our fortunes, and our sacred honor" (Declaration of Independence). Later he said, "I shall need, too, the favor of that Being in whose hands we are, who led our fathers, as Israel of old, from their native land and planted them in a country flowing with all the necessaries and comforts of life; who has covered our infancy with His providence and our riper years with His wisdom and power" (Second Inaugural Address). Jefferson genuinely acknowledged divine transcendence. It all fit so well with the ideal of chosen nationhood, manifest destiny, evangelical values and deistic civil piety.

The facts are clear. America was born in unusual historical circumstances, it was blessed with extraordinarily talented leaders in its formative years, it was a land which contained vast natural resources and a temperate climate, it enjoyed a splendid isolation from the Old World while it experimented with new republican ideas and institutions, and it successfully endured the furnace of civil war and actually came through the time of testing stronger than before. In short there was substance to the half-grudging, half-admiring remark made by Otto von Bismarck in 1898 when he received news of the American romp in Cuba in the war with Spain. The retired German chancellor allegedly growled that there seemed to be a special Providence which looked after drunkards, fools and the United States of America![59]

To oversimplify, being an American in the nineteenth century was to vote for causes that advanced democracy and to behave in general accordance with evangelical values. This was the essence of civil religion in that era (if, in reality,

there was one during that period); it was virtually synonymous with evangelical Christianity and democratic politics.
At the same time, however, an element of deist civil religion
lingered in the wings, always willing to play a supportive
role, but waiting for an opportunity to steal the show.

The Waning of Evangelical Vitality   Unfortunately for the
vitality of the evangelical faith, toward the end of the century
it entered a period of cultural captivity. In the wake of the
new immigration, the problems of urbanization and the advent of theological liberalism, the evangelical consensus
gradually became the Protestant Establishment. The change
from consensus to establishment Christianity was both an
expression of satisfaction with the status quo and a determination by the old mainline Protestant denominations to
make peace at home and to brace themselves for the threat
from without—foreigners, anarchists, Catholics, Jews and
German rationalists (the last-named group bringing with
them higher criticism and theological liberalism). Also, in
this same era the new ideologies of Marxism and Darwinism
began to challenge the Christian faith. Most significantly,
during the years 1890 to 1914 the Protestant Establishment
cohabited with corporate capitalism and began to procreate.
Their miscegenetic offspring were materialism, militant
nationalism and a much more broadly-based, much less
evangelically-influenced civil religion.

For their part, many evangelicals found it difficult to harmonize the historic Christian faith of the Bible with an increasingly pluralistic society. Whereas in previous generations to be an American meant to hold evangelical values,
this became less and less true in the years after 1890. Newly
arrived immigrants no longer pushed on to the frontier, there
to be assimilated into American life, but instead tended to
settle in the large cities and retain their old ethnic religions
and ways—ones that were quite different from traditional
evangelicalism.

Thus, in the late nineteenth and early twentieth centuries

the evangelical consensus became the Protestant Establishment, the chosen nation theme now smacked of superiority and condescension, the mission of American democracy turned into strident nationalism and the philosophy of progress was transformed into blatant materialism. In the process civil religion became more and more an expression of American tribal ethnocentrism.

Of course a more purely deistic civil faith existed alongside, and in some ways was a functional part of, the evangelical consensus cum civil religion all through the nineteenth century. This preference for the civic theology of the Enlightenment was most obvious in the intellectual community before the turn of the century. Then, when the fundamentalist-modernist controversy of the 1920s shattered the old Protestant Establishment, a new and more latitudinarian civil religion moved to the forefront of American civic piety.

During World War 1 and more especially World War 2 this broader and essentially deistic civil religion helped to mobilize an increasingly pluralistic nation against foreign enemies. After the Second World War civil religion experienced another major upsurge as American political leaders struggled anew with the problem of national unity—a unity seriously threatened by religious and cultural pluralism, growing racial and political unrest, the alienation of youth from the system and the ethnic revivals. In the process of trying to meet the ever-increasing need for national unity in a country with an ever-decreasing amount of religious and cultural cohesion, the base of American civil religion gradually was expanded. During the course of American history its umbrella has been enlarged from evangelical consensus to Protestantism-in-general, to Christianity-in-general, to the Judeo-Christian-tradition-in-general to deism-in-general.[60]

When G. K. Chesterton recorded that he had encountered "a nation with the soul of a church" on his journey to the United States, little did he realize that he was visiting a country in the throes of radical change—culturally, socially and religiously. As a foreigner he no doubt could perceive some things which Americans closer to the scene could not, but on the other hand, he was to some extent a prisoner of his own era. What he described was the remains of the old America which was on the threshold of the most chaotic and fast-paced decade in its history. America in 1921 was much more like it was fifty years before than it would be fifty years later.

The American civil religion of the nineteenth century was informed by evangelical Christian values and an evangelical lifestyle. Even in 1920 civil religion reflected much of its historic development in an evangelically-oriented age. Fifty years before, evangelical Christianity was still virile and dominated the national civil faith, but by 1920 it was no longer the ascendant moral ideology of the nation. At the same time, the country's civil religion was beginning to change so that it would mirror its diverse constituency. Now, by the 1970s it has become a highly generalized civil faith because the country is an extremely pluralistic society in terms of religion, ethics, values and lifestyle. The days of the evangelical consensus now appear to be over.

Chesterton observed a civil religion which still reflected much of the certainty and optimism of the previous century. Fifty years later it was much more difficult to identify with precision what the religion of the republic was. After the midtwentieth-century civil religion was much less certain, less dogmatic, less demanding in its requirements and less sure of its legitimate parameters. A decade of dissension and drift in the 1960s had taken its toll. America entered the 1970s with its former confidence in the future shaken as never before in its history. Anxiety replaced hope as the dominant emotion in the hearts and lives of many of its citizens.

The next chapter will survey the development of American civil religion in the period following World War 1. In so doing, it will give special attention to the role of evangelical Christianity—positive and negative—in the religious and political life of the nation since that time. This examination of the modern American search for national meaning and purpose will serve as the basis for an in-depth assessment of the beneficial and detrimental features of civil religion, especially from an evangelical Christian perspective.

3
ONE NATION UNDER GOD: THE NEW SEARCH FOR NATIONAL MEANING

The Protestant Establishment was seriously threatened by the changes in late nineteenth-century American life. God's New Israel was beset by invasion from without and spiritual erosion from within. Dangerous foreign ideologies such as Marxism, higher criticism and Darwinism were beginning to sink roots in the fertile soil of the New World. Hordes of immigrants continued to pour into the promised land, but now they were new types of people who did not know the "God of our forefathers"—Italians, Greeks, Slavs, Hungarians, Jews, Orientals—who were Roman Catholic, Eastern Orthodox, Jewish and occasionally even Buddhist in their religious beliefs. The Protestant churches were stunned by the enormity of the urban problems resulting from the rapid progress of industrialization. Such things as substandard housing, disease, poverty, unemployment, crime and disintegration of family life taxed to the breaking point the resources of the churches' charitable outreach.

At the same time, American Christianity became polarized over how to respond to these problems. The social gospel faction argued that the state must take a leading role in reform and strike at the bastion of economic privilege which was helping to perpetuate social ills. The more conservative group tended to downplay social reform and emphasized a gospel of individual salvation and personal piety. As theological liberalism invaded the ranks of the social gospelers, the rift between the two widened and the way was opened for the acrimonious fundamentalist-modernist controversy of the 1920s. But before 1914 calm still prevailed on the surface of American Protestantism, and many still clung to the fond hope that the better world of the kingdom of God lay just beyond the horizon.

World War 1 and the Breakup of the Protestant Establishment   The outbreak of war in faraway Europe in 1914 was destined to transform the nature of the American civil religion. The movement for world peace which had enlisted the support of prominent church people in the prewar years was stopped dead in its tracks. The thundering "guns of August" and the "rape" of Belgium dashed into a thousand pieces the millennial expectation of many evangelical Protestants that the kingdom of God was about to be ushered into the earthly theater of human history. The British propaganda apparatus succeeded in convincing a substantial number of church leaders that the Allies were engaged in a "holy war." American business and banking interests supplied them with generous quantities of war materials and inexhaustible lines of credit, and more and more notables climbed aboard the preparedness bandwagon as the conflict dragged on. Thus, when the final break with Germany came in early 1917, the American masses swarmed with boundless enthusiasm to the colors to take up arms against the unspeakable horrors of Kaiserism and on behalf of national righteousness.

The churches played a key role in whipping up public enthusiasm for the war effort.[1] The molders of religious opinion developed a "theology of the struggle" in terms of "light versus darkness, virtue versus sin, humanity versus autocracy, civilization versus chaos, and God versus the devil."[2] Clerics blessed the war and the instruments of terror as necessary to carry out the will of God, and religious organizations entered willingly into the service of the government to stimulate patriotism and self-sacrifice, promote the sale of Liberty Bonds, recruit soldiers for the army, encourage conservation of food, suppress subversive ideas and keep up morale on the home front and among the fighting men. Church leaders freely disseminated the grossest types of war propaganda, and many of them fully agreed with the sentiments that evangelist Billy Sunday expressed in a prayer he offered early in 1918 before the House of Representatives in Washington, D.C.:

> Thou knowest, O Lord, that we are in a life-and-death struggle with one of the most infamous, vile, greedy, avaricious, bloodthirsty, sensual, and vicious nations that has ever disgraced the pages of history. . . . We pray Thee that Thou wilt make bare Thy mighty arm and beat back that great pack of hungry, wolfish Huns, whose fangs drip with blood and gore. We pray Thee that the stars in their courses and the winds and waves may fight against them.[3]

Any attempt to point the finger at America's own shortcomings (such as the time when Presbyterian mission executive Robert E. Speer called attention in a speech to broken treaties, bad labor conditions and race prejudice) was immediately drowned out by a chorus of patriotic recrimination.[4] The minority of ministers who opposed the war, expressed concern for conscientious objectors or espoused pacifist views of any kind were frequently hounded from their pulpits and some were prosecuted under the wartime Espionage and Sedition Acts. With scarcely a whimper of protest the churches stood by as constitutionally-guaranteed civil liberties were swept away by mass hysteria and official action.

Drawn by the seductive allurements of nationalism, Christians gave themselves over unreservedly to sanctifying the American cause in the war. In clear conscience, Protestant and Roman Catholic dignitaries alike could express publicly: "The man who is disloyal to the flag is disloyal to Christianity; the State must be obeyed under pain of incurring the guilt of mutiny against God," and, "We must keep the flag and the

Cross together, for they are both working for the same ends."[5]
Ray Abrams' indictment of the churches during World War 1
is truly damning:

> The church leaders, in spite of their priestly claim to depth
> of spiritual insight and knowledge of ethical values, dis-
> played no such superior quality of moral judgment as has
> been assumed.... The clergy were swept from their moor-
> ings in exactly the same way as were many of those un-
> tutored minds who made no pretension to holiness or lov-
> ing one's neighbor or knowledge of God's will.[6]

As American evangelicals plunged wholeheartedly into the
"Great Crusade" for democracy and against Prussian militarism and despotism, they laid aside every semblance of
prophetic witness. Cracks had already begun to appear in
Protestant ranks long before 1914, and according to historian
George Marsden "the ancient ideal of a Christian society had
become little more than an illusionary superstructure only
partly masking revolutionary changes in the basic intellectual assumptions, values, and social patterns of the culture."[7]
All that really remained was a facade of moralism and sentiment, and the abdication of moral responsibility during the
conflict insured that Protestants would not be able to recover
their position of spiritual solidarity and leadership within
American society.

The war years saw a distinct erosion in the Protestant
Establishment and the emergence of a new phenomenon, the
incorporation of Roman Catholics and Jews into the politico-
religious consensus. Leaders of both communions rallied
with vigor to the national cause. A few days after Congress
had declared war, the Catholic archbishops under the aegis
of James Cardinal Gibbons unanimously pledged their support: "Our people, as ever, will rise as one man to serve the
nation." The cardinal pronounced that a citizen's primary
duty is "loyalty to country" and "it is exhibited by an absolute and unreserved obedience to his country." Praising the
members of Congress who voted to declare war in 1917,
Gibbons called them "the instruments of God in guiding us

in our civic duties."[8] Endorsing the Third Liberty Loan, New York Rabbi Stephen S. Wise proclaimed: "I would have the members of the churches, Christian and Jewish, alike, stand foremost among the citizens of America furthering the high war aims of our nation."[9]

The expansion of the national religious consensus was exemplified excellently by the published letter of Vincent J. Toole, a Catholic chaplain serving in France, to Theodore Roosevelt. The cleric asserted that if even "a single individual Catholic" back home remained uncommitted to the righteousness of our cause, he was a traitor and should be dealt with accordingly. "Nearly fifty percent of the army under fire today is Catholic. Many of our best officers and men are Jews." According to Toole, "It is an inspiring sight to see the spirit of real fraternity there among the troops in the field —Catholic and Protestant and Jew standing as one man presenting a solid front to a common enemy." Perceptively he observed that an "important by-product" of the war would be a better spirit of mutual understanding back home.[10] In other words, in the future the United States would no longer be exclusively a Protestant nation, but one in which all faiths would share equally.

The Advance of Secularism in the 1920s According to Sydney Ahlstrom, the war had been a tremendous stimulus to piety among the Protestants: "Never had the churches been better attended, never had so many members been busily involved in the country's life and work, never had the general public's judgments of religion been so affirmative or their generosity with money more apparent."[11] Thus, church leaders assumed that the momentum of the Great Crusade would send them on to final victory over evil, and with the defeat of Germany the long-anticipated new world order of peace, justice and democracy finally would come to fruition. The Protestant Establishment, committed to the ideals of social reform, world peace and church unity, lined up solidly behind its Presbyterian messiah Woodrow Wilson in his endeavor to create the League of Nations, an international agency that would prevent future outbreaks of war. Hoping to coordinate their benevolent efforts, many ecclesiastical leaders united in a grandiose (but unsuccessful) campaign known as the Interchurch World Movement to secure money and workers for the social service and missionary outreach of the various denominations.[12]

However, their constituency had wearied of involvement, sacrifice and grand ideals, and longed for the tranquility of normalcy. Only one social issue remained that could capture the imagination of both laissez-faire individualist business elements and the advocates of an other-worldly gospel. That was Prohibition which after World War 1 became in effect a surrogate for the social gospel. Moreover, because the Protestant Establishment had failed to sink deep roots among the urban masses and new immigrants, it became increasingly middle class and small town in its social outlook and membership. Throughout the country church attendance declined, while the denominations were torn by acrimonious strife between the so-called modernists and fundamentalists. It was as Ahlstrom observed, a genuine "time of crisis for both the Protestant Establishment and the historic evangelicalism which undergirded it."[13]

Politically, religion was regarded as a bulwark against radicalism, and the enthusiasm for patriotic Americanism which had animated rank-and-file Protestants during the war was channeled into repressive actions against nonconformists of every stripe. This was reflected in such matters as the Red Scare of 1919-20, nativist pressure to limit immigration to peoples from Northern and Western Europe, Ku Klux Klan intimidation of Negroes and Catholics, and the wide variety of Jim Crow and anti-Semitic measures which substantially restricted the participation of these groups in American political, economic and social life. Wilsonian internationalism was rudely cast aside in favor of a return to isolationism, while the average American was concerned more with pleasure and accumulating material possessions than with the welfare of neighbors at home and abroad.

These developments sapped the vitality of the Protestant faith and contributed immeasurably to its demise as the dominant religious force in American life.[14] The old moral beliefs of Middle America came under fire as the intellectual elite formulated a new morality based upon the premise that religion should defer to science. The evolution controversy, highlighted by the disastrous Scopes Trial of 1925, called attention to the vast chasm that had opened between the defenders of orthodoxy and the champions of the new science. With the failure to secure legislation against the teaching of evolution in the public schools and unable to check the growing impact of industrialization and urbanization on American life, many evangelicals placed all the blame for social ills on Demon Rum. But, Prohibition proved not to be the panacea its proponents had said it would be, and many believers retreated from active social involvement into a shell of monastic pietism where correct theology, private prayer and personal evangelism were seen as the only ways of coping with growing social problems. At the same time, many Christians were caught up in the spiraling affluence and materialism of the era and like their secular compatriots they looked upon possessions and money as a sign of success and God's approval.

Because this was a period of increasing cultural, ethnic and religious heterogeneity and the debilitating fundamentalist-modernist dispute set brother against brother, the Protestant Establishment began to disintegrate. Many church leaders, according to Ahlstrom, became "sharply aware that their ancient sway over the nation's moral life was threatened."[15] The bitter struggle between fundamentalists and modernists essentially discredited evangelical Christianity in the eyes of the American public, much like the "Babylonian Captivity" had done to the medieval papacy in its day. Deeply divided in their own ranks and unable to impose their values upon society in such matters as Prohibition, Sunday observance and evolution, the orthodox stood helpless in the face of the militant onslaught of secularism. After dominating American society and culture in the previous century, evangelical Christians now took on the earmarks of an unimportant and despised subculture. Like blacks in America, they were ignored in history textbooks and virtually disappeared from the mass media's consideration during the generation following 1925.[16] As Ahlstrom sums up the situation: "Modern thought and social change were slowly bringing down the curtains on the 'great century' of American evangelicalism."[17] The twenties marked the crucial transition in American religious history from the Protestant Establishment to the civil religious consensus.

Toward a New Consensus   It was evident by the time of the Great Depression that a significant shift in the history of national devotion had occurred. For the first time Americans became genuinely aware of alternative ideological options, such as socialism and communism. The transcendent, providential character of America began to fade from view. Civil religion became for many either an ironic form of national idolatry or a naive belief in progress and by the 1950s was increasingly invoked as an antidote to social criticism.[18]

During the interwar years religious life displayed a substantial measure of vigor but little unity in any meaningful sense. There was a kind of Protestant liberal establishment which exercised a considerable amount of influence in the administration of Herbert Hoover, a committed Quaker who had earlier served as a vice president of the Federal Council of Churches. Relations between the president and the FCC cooled, however, as the council increasingly criticized capitalism during the depression.[19] But the liberals regained their position of prestige after the advent of the New Deal. Pacifism and the social gospel reappeared as formidable forces after their eclipse in the 1920s, while the ecumenical movement grew in strength and significance as several denominational mergers occurred and closer ties were established with church groups abroad. Neo-orthodoxy brought about a renewal of concern for doctrinal matters and other biblical themes in some quarters.

Religious minority groups also experienced a resurgence. White fundamentalists, who had retreated to lick their wounds, were regrouping and would re-enter the mainstream of religious life in the 1940s and 1950s with the evangelical message. The black churches were largely evangelical and constituted the decisive factor in enabling Negroes to survive and develop a distinctive culture in spite of their exclusion from most of the amenities of American life. During the 1920s the Roman Catholic minority was forced to fight a rear-guard action against nativist bigotry, but in the 1930s their position in public life was appreciably enhanced through their involvement in the labor movement and the Democratic Party.[20]

Although a confessional consensus no longer existed, Americans were still by and large a religious people and hence civil religion took up the slack and bound them together. Calvin Coolidge, who succeeded to the presidency in 1923 when Warren G. Harding suddenly died, excellently reflected the national faith which was emerging in this period. In his memoirs Coolidge described how, when he received word of Harding's passing, before leaving his bedroom in the family home in Vermont to go take the oath of office, he "knelt down and, with the same prayer with which I have since approached the altar of the church, asked God to bless the American people and give me power to serve them." Shortly after his arrival in the capital he attended a worship service at the First Congregational Church where he took communion. Even though he belonged to no church at all, the congregation decided this sufficed as a profession of faith and voted him into its membership.[21]

Coolidge confessed that one was placed in the White House not because of his own exertions or merit; instead, "Some power outside and beyond him becomes manifest through him. As he contemplates the workings of his office, he comes to realize with an increasing sense of humility that he is but an instrument in the hands of God."[22] After being elected president in 1924, Coolidge declared in his inaugural speech that the country was "an example of tranquility at home, a patron of tranquility abroad" and the government was "aware of its might but obedient to its conscience." He ended his remarks with a stirring civil religion appeal:

America seeks no earthly empire built on blood and force. No ambition, no temptation, lures her to thought of foreign dominions. The legions which she sends forth are armed, not with the sword, but with the cross. The higher state to which she seeks the allegiance of all mankind is not of human, but of divine origin. She cherishes no purpose save to merit the favor of Almighty God.[23]

As noted in the previous chapter, American presidents from the very beginning of the republic freely utilized religious imagery and language on public occasions. Some of them were merely pro forma in nature while others represented a genuine, heartfelt faith. But with the appearance of the civil religion consensus they took on much more significance. These expressions, consciously or unconsciously, now served to motivate Americans and to enlist their energies on behalf of national causes and policies in a largely nonevangelical context.

Roosevelt and the Crisis of World War 2 Coolidge's public religiosity met the needs of an era of tranquility; Franklin D. Roosevelt found civil religion indispensable in bringing the country through the crisis of World War 2. According to his intimate adviser Samuel Rosenman, the Episcopalian Roosevelt was not a regular churchgoer but was "a deeply religious man." He "felt a veneration for his Creator which expressed itself often." The references to God which appear so frequently in his speeches were prompted by this feeling. Rosenman maintains that the president's deep concern for other peoples, even the meanest and lowliest, "had its roots in his religious conviction of the innate dignity of every human being."[24]

Roosevelt recognized the threat of the gathering clouds of war to American freedom and concluded that the country must shore up its defenses and work for collective security with other peace-loving nations. In his Annual Message to Congress on January 4, 1939, the president stressed that the storms from abroad directly challenged three institutions indispensable to Americans—religion, democracy and international good faith. He referred to the first as the source of the other two because "religion by teaching man his relationship to God, gives the individual a sense of his own dignity and teaches him to respect himself by respecting his neighbors." The three complemented and supported each other in a modern civilization. Where freedom of religion had been attacked, it had come from sources opposed to democracy, and the spirit of free worship had disappeared where democracy had been overthrown. In this context he argued:

An ordering of society which relegates religion, democracy and good faith among nations to the background can find no place within it for the ideals of the Prince of Peace. The United States rejects such an ordering, and retains its ancient faith.

There comes a time in the affairs of men when they must prepare to defend not their homes alone but the tenets of faith and humanity on which their churches, their governments and their very civilization are founded. The defense of religion, of democracy and of good faith among nations is all the same fight. To save one we must now make up our minds to save all.[25]

Similar views were expressed in his State of the Union Address two years later when he pointed to the vision of a new moral order in the world where each person would possess the four freedoms—freedom of speech and expression, freedom to worship God in his own way, freedom from want and freedom from fear. This would be attainable only through the cooperation of free countries working together in a civilized society. Roosevelt concluded by affirming: "This nation has placed its destiny in the hands and heads and hearts of millions of free men and women; and its faith in freedom under the guidance of God," and he pledged that the United States would support those people everywhere who were struggling for human rights.[26]

Once the United States was drawn into the hostilities, the chief executive on numerous occasions appealed to his countrymen's faith in God and sense of national purpose and destiny. In his War Message to Congress after Pearl Harbor in 1941, he eloquently denounced the Japanese treachery and reaffirmed his faith in America's "righteous might," declaring that, "with confidence in our armed forces—with the unbounding determination of our people—we will gain the inevitable triumph—so help us God."[27] Roosevelt asked the nation to set aside New Year's Day, 1942 as a day of prayer for divine guidance, and in his Annual Message to Congress on January 6, 1942, he maintained that "the world is too small to provide adequate 'living room' for both Hitler and God." While the enemy was guided by brutal cynicism and contempt for the human race, the Americans were fighting to cleanse the world of ancient ills and were inspired by the faith that "God created man in His own image." Further:

> We are fighting, as our fathers have fought, to uphold the doctrine that all men are equal in the sight of God. Those on the other side are striving to destroy this deep belief and to create a world in their own image, a world of tyranny and cruelty and serfdom.
>
> This is the conflict that day and night now pervades our lives. No compromise can end that conflict. There never has been and never can be a successful compromise between good and evil. Only total victory can reward the champions of tolerance and decency and freedom and faith.[28]

One of Roosevelt's most moving public statements was his D-Day prayer broadcast to the nation on June 6, 1944, as American troops were storming the beaches of Normandy. Instead of delivering a speech on that historic occasion, he read a simple civil prayer in which he asked his "Fellow Americans" to join:

Almighty God: Our sons, pride of our Nation, this day have set upon a mighty endeavor, a struggle to preserve our Republic, our religion, and our civilization, and to set free a suffering humanity.

Lead them straight and true: give strength to their arms, stoutness to their hearts, steadfastness in their faith.

They will need Thy blessings. Their road will be long and hard. For the enemy is strong. He may hurl back our forces. Success may not come with rushing speed, but we shall return again and again; and we know that by Thy grace, and by the righteousness of our cause, our sons will triumph. . . .

Some will never return. Embrace these, Father, and receive them, Thy heroic servants, into Thy kingdom.

And for us at home . . . help us, Almighty God, to rededicate ourselves in renewed faith in Thee in this hour of great sacrifice. . . .

O Lord, give us faith. Give us faith in Thee, faith in our sons, faith in each other, faith in our united crusade. . . .

With Thy blessing, we shall prevail over the unholy forces of our enemy. Help us to conquer the apostles of greed and racial arrogance. Lead us to the saving of our country, and with our sister nations into a world unity that will spell a sure peace.[29]

Thus, the president led in an effort to unite the people of the country in a common faith designed to fortify them for the contest against godless, inhuman fascism. In a similar manner two events serve to illustrate how the civil religion consensus assisted in winning support for the war effort and how it consciously incorporated the three major faiths. On February 3, 1943 the *Dorchester*, a troopship bound for Europe, was torpedoed off Greenland. Four army chaplains, two Protestant, one Roman Catholic and one Jewish, together passed out life jackets, and when all were gone, gave their own to soldiers who had none. They were last seen standing on the deck, arms locked and praying as the ship went down. Hailed as an inspirational example—"men of all faiths can be proud that these men of different faiths died together"— they were posthumously awarded Distinguished Service Crosses in a widely publicized ceremony.[30]

On May 21, 1944 a festival of national solidarity called "I Am an American Day," was staged in New York's Central Park. Over one million people gathered to watch 150,000 new citizens take the Oath of Allegiance for the first time and to hear speeches by various dignitaries. Representatives of the three faiths—Catholic prelate Francis W. Walsh, Episcopal bishop William T. Manning and Jewish rabbi Stephen S. Wise—delivered prayers calling for victory and peace. Rabbi Wise prayed that American war aims would "prove worthy of Thy blessing," and pleaded for a "spirit of deepened and ennobled loyalty to our country" and "a spirit of brotherliness to one another across and beyond all barriers of race and faith." Circuit court Judge Learned Hand told the assembled multitudes that they as Americans were there to affirm faith in liberty. He stressed that the "spirit of liberty" moves people to seek to understand the minds and interests of others, and it "is the spirit of Him who, nearly two thousand years ago, taught mankind that lesson it has never learned but has never quite forgotten; that there may be a kingdom where the least shall be heard and considered side by side with the greatest."[31] Such are the affirmations of a faceless, nonevangelical civil religion.

Truman and the Cold War Roosevelt's death in April 1945 brought Harry S. Truman to the White House. Although nominally a Baptist, Truman was actually more of a general Protestant in the civil religion tradition and, like his predecessor, he appealed to the civil religion consensus. In his first speech to Congress, Truman utilized the language of civil piety which people were accustomed to hearing: "America must assist suffering humanity back along the path of peaceful progress. . . . America has become one of the

most powerful forces for good on earth. We must keep it so."
He concluded with the prayer of Solomon: "Give therefore
Thy servant an understanding heart to judge Thy people,
that I may discern between good and bad: for who is able to
judge this Thy so great people?" Then he asked, "Only to
be a good and faithful servant of my Lord and my people."[32]

The Cold War brought a new challenge to the nation, and
Truman channeled the civil religion into the struggle against
the communist menace. In his 1949 Inaugural Address, he
set forth a four-point program for combating the "false philosophy" of communism. At the same time he proclaimed
"the essential principles of the faith by which we live," that
is, "all men have a right to equal justice under the law and
equal opportunity to share in the common good." All have
the right to freedom of thought and expression and are
equal because "they are created in the image of God." Then
he listed a number of differences between democracy
and communism and stressed that these involved "material
well-being, human dignity, and the right to believe in and
worship God." He ended on a note of hope: "Steadfast in our
faith in the Almighty, we will advance toward a world where
man's freedom is secure. . . . With God's help, the future of
mankind will be assured in a world of justice, harmony and
peace."[33]

Truman explained to a delegation from the Augustana
Lutheran Church a few days before the outbreak of the Kore-
an War in 1950 that the United States was "the leader of the
moral forces of the world." Further, Americans believed that
the law under which they lived was "God-given" and that
their "traditions have come from Moses at Sinai and Jesus on
the Mount." Whereas they endeavor "to live by the law,"
the Russian communists "do not believe in a moral code,"
and they "even go so far as to say there is no Supreme Being."[34] In a speech at the cornerstone laying of the New York
Avenue Presbyterian Church in 1951, the president maintained that "religion should establish moral standards for the
conduct of our whole Nation, at home and abroad." He went

on to say: "Our religious faith gives us the answer to the false beliefs of Communism. . . . I have the feeling that God has created us and brought us to our present position of power and strength for some great purpose." It is America's duty "to defend the spiritual values—the moral code—against the vast forces of evil that seek to destroy them."[35]

In effect Truman was espousing the old concept of national mission, an idea that still possessed considerable potency and appeal, and was harnessing it to the American effort in the East-West conflict. However, this ideal was now emptied of its evangelical Christian content and was made more generalized in character. Others of the period, like General Douglas MacArthur, carried the argument further. He agreed with Truman's view that America rested upon a foundation of morality derived from religion, and that communism rejected the sanctity of moral law and "worships as its only god the power to suppress the Divine heritage of man." But the great "Proconsul of the East" adopted a stance that endeared him to all those who had mourned the passing of the Protestant Establishment. Labeling "atheistic Communism" as the "greatest scourge of mankind," MacArthur maintained that there could be "no compromise"—it must be all or nothing. To counterbalance those who sought "to convert us to a form of socialistic endeavor leading directly to the path of Communist slavery," he offered patriotism and Christianity:

> Our greatest hope and faith rests upon two mighty symbols—the Cross and the Flag; the one based upon those immutable teachings which provide the spiritual strength to persevere along the course which is just and right—the other based upon the invincible will that human freedom shall not perish from the earth. These are the mighty bulwarks against the advance of those atheistic predatory forces which seek to destroy the spirituality of the human mind and to enslave the human body.[36]

The armed forces chaplaincy was also a noteworthy feature of the new civil religion consensus during this period. The

Reverend Edward L. R. Elson, a prominent evangelical cleric and former chaplain, contends that during World War 2 the American military establishment provided for religion as no other nation in all history has provided for the spiritual needs of its personnel. Chaplains, he noted, were drawn from "all phases of our religious culture" on a proportional basis, while the government supplied them with chapels and equipment and paid their salaries.[37] The rationale for this was that the government was obligated to give people in uniform who were away from their regular homes and places of worship the opportunity for the "free exercise of religion" guaranteed by the First Amendment. One of the major functions of the chaplaincy that emerged in the Cold War years was "character guidance," a program of counseling and basic morality talks to help individuals in the service develop a sense of responsibility "as set forth in the Moral Law and the Natural Law." Accordingly, an army manual of 1950 attested that religion contributed to strength of character and buttressed the basic teaching of democracy. It was "a vital interest to all who would protect and preserve our way of life," or to put it another way, religion-in-general was to exercise a basically conservative function.[38]

The Golden Age of Modern American Civil Religion: The 1950s The flowering of modern American civil religion was in the Eisenhower years. Because patriotism and religion were being utilized as weapons in the ideological struggle with "godless international communism," the central position of the civic faith in American life was enhanced. The pluralism that dominated the religious landscape determined that the expressions of religiosity would be broad and vague enough to encompass the adherents of the three major faiths (really four, as representatives of the Eastern Orthodox churches came to be included in public functions), and all those who acknowledged a Supreme Being. Only freethinkers, agnostics and atheistic humanists now seemed to lie outside the civil religion pale.

The national mood was congenial to an outpouring of religiosity, and examples of it abounded. In 1952 Congress instructed the president to proclaim annually a National Day of Prayer. A Prayer for Peace movement spread across the country in the early 1950s and even the post office cancelled stamps with the slogan *Pray for Peace*. The indefatigable Abram Vereide, head of International Christian Leadership, promoted the prayer breakfast idea among the leaders of government and business, culminating in 1953 with the first annual Presidential (now National) Prayer Breakfast.

A *New York Herald Tribune* editor rallied popular support for issuance of a postage stamp bearing the motto *In God We Trust* that would publicize to the world that America was a nation of faith. This was followed by legislation in 1955 mandating it to appear on all currency and coins (it had merely been authorized during the Civil War). In 1956 Congress established it as the official national motto. The American Legion initiated an annual Back to God observance in 1951 to commemorate the Four Chaplains and increase the awareness of God in people's daily lives. In 1953 a prestigious collection of leaders from the three faiths launched a short-lived "Foundation for Religious Action in the Social and Civil Order" to unite all people who believed in a Supreme Being in a spiritual and ideological counteroffensive against communism. Religion in American Life, founded in 1949 and backed by forty denominational groups representing the various faiths, busily engaged in advertising religion and brotherhood.

The most dramatic display of growing public religiosity was the change in the Pledge of Allegiance. Written in 1892 by Baptist minister Francis Bellamy, its usage had grown in popularity through the years. In 1945 it was made the official national oath by congressional action. Early in 1954 a minister in Washington complained that there was no difference between the American pledge and one the Soviets might use because God was not mentioned in it. At once Senator Homer Ferguson and Representative Louis C. Rabaut, both of Michigan, took up the challenge and in a few days rushed a resolution through Congress adding the words from Lincoln's Gettysburg Address "under God" to the pledge. Roman Catholic backing for the modification was as strong as Protestant support and a Knights of Columbus official even claimed he had suggested the idea to Rabaut. When President Eisenhower signed the bill on Flag Day, he declared:

From this day forward, the millions of our school children will daily proclaim in every city and town, every village and rural school house, the dedication of our nation and our people to the Almighty. To anyone who truly loves America, nothing could be more inspiring than to contemplate this rededication of our youth, on each school morning, to our country's true meaning.[39]

Dwight D. Eisenhower more than anyone else symbolized the religious temper of the 1950s. Of humble origins he was reared in a devout, pietistic, Brethren environment in Kansas that inculcated in him the virtues of integrity, courage, hard work, self-reliance and an unshakable belief in the Bible which he read and memorized. In his mature years he showed little concern for formal religion, but an interest in Christianity seemed to revive when he assumed the duties of leadership in World War 2. He acknowledged the awesome responsibilities that Providence had placed upon him and interpreted the conflict as a "crusade" to uphold democracy and religious values. When he ran for the presidency in 1952, he conducted a campaign reminiscent of his World War 2 crusade in Europe, but this one was moral and religious in tone—a crusade against communism abroad and corruption, bureaucratic regimentation and creeping socialism at home.[40]

Although not a church member, Eisenhower had internalized the Bible and made it a vital part of his thought and expression. His brother Milton maintains that he was "a deeply religious man" who regularly attended church during his military career but was never stationed anywhere long enough to sink roots. He disliked denominationalism

and ritualism because they were merely outward manifestations, whereas he recognized the true significance of religion as being in the mind and heart. The general said in 1948,
"I am the most intensely religious man I know. Nobody goes
through six years of war without a faith. That does not mean
that I adhere to any sect."[41]

The inauguration set the tone for the direction which civil
religion would take during the Eisenhower administration.
On the morning of January 20, 1953 the president-elect,
cabinet and their families attended church where Eisenhower "sought strength in prayer and in the Word of God
for his overwhelming new responsibilities." The mood of the
service was, according to Dr. Elson who officiated, that of
"placing the destiny of the nation in God's hands." The new
president then stopped by his room in the Statler Hotel, composed a brief prayer and proceeded to the Capitol for the
inaugural ceremony.

After taking the oath of office he offered the "little private
prayer" he had written, an action unique in the annals of
presidential inaugurations. In it he besought God to "make
full and complete our dedication to the service of the people
in this throng and their fellow citizens everywhere." He
asked for power to discern right from wrong, that American
words and actions be governed by this principle and by the
laws of the land, and that a concern exist for all the people
regardless of their station, race or calling. Then he requested
that cooperation be the mutual aim of those who hold to dif-
fering political faiths, "so that all may work for the good of
our beloved country and Thy glory." The inaugural address
itself was a call for spiritual rededication and moral renewal.
"Whatever America hopes to bring to pass in the world must
first come to pass in the heart of America," the president
intoned. The peace this country was seeking was "the practice and fulfillment of our whole faith among ourselves and
in our dealings with others," one that could be regarded as a
way of life, hope for the brave and the work that awaits all
Americans.[42]

Eisenhower also demonstrated a public faith. A few days after the inauguration he was baptized and joined the National Presbyterian Church in Washington, where he worshiped regularly thereafter. In a precedent-setting move he attended the first Presidential Prayer Breakfast and witnessed to the power and meaning of prayer in his life. He initiated the practice of opening cabinet meetings with prayer, an action which gained him the commendation of the Catholic (Jesuit) weekly *America* for his forthrightness in testifying to the "realization of our dependence on God's providence."[43]

The chief executive frequently dispatched greetings to or spoke to church bodies and clerical delegations. One such group came from the National Association of Evangelicals, representing the new generation of orthodox Protestants who were endeavoring to move back into the mainstream of American religious life. He discussed with them the need for a moral and religious base to guarantee the continuance of American freedom and signed a document which called for a national reaffirmation of faith in God (the Author of man's freedom), repentance from sin and a new dedication to bringing liberty to the world.[44] When a McCarthy Committee staff member made some sensational charges about communists among the clergy, Eisenhower responded with a firm statement expressing his confidence in the churches as the "citadels of our faith in individual freedom and human dignity." This faith was the source of the nation's spiritual strength, which in turn was "our matchless armor in our world-wide struggle against the forces of godless tyranny and oppression."[45]

Eisenhower's political theology was epitomized in a comment at the 1953 Prayer Breakfast: the country was founded on one idea—the "simple basic truth" that "every free government is embedded solidly in a deeply felt religious faith or it makes no sense."[46] He reiterated this before the young people at the World Christian Endeavor Convention, where he called upon people to remember "the spiritual base that underlies all free government, else we shall surely fail."[47] Naturally his admirers, such as Billy Graham or Edward Elson (who put out a book celebrating "America's spiritual recovery"), could scarcely restrain their enthusiasm about the upsurge of presidential religiosity.

Others were not so sure, especially the perceptive William Lee Miller, who penned a number of articles that were eventually collected in a book entitled *Piety along the Potomac.* He suggested that President Eisenhower, like many Americans, was a "fervent believer in a very vague religion." He talked about "believing" or "faith" independent of its object ("the devoted people meeting here believe, first of all, always in faith," so Eisenhower told the Evanston assembly of the World Council of Churches); emphasized feeling rather than content or meaning ("our form of government has no sense unless it is founded in a deeply religious faith—and I don't care what it is"); recommended religion for its utility ("faith is the mightiest force that man has at his command"); connected this generalized religion with the nation's "foundation"; and differentiated America from the communist world on the basis that this land was religious while the Soviets were atheistic. Religion appeared to be little more than an endorsement of the aims and purposes of America, "the mightiest power which God has yet seen fit to put upon his footstool." In essence, the values which sprang from this commitment to religion-in-general were values-in-general, or as Eisenhower once put it: "Honesty, decency, fairness, service—all that sort of thing."[48]

The President As Priest   The problem, however, is deeper than mere superficial political theology. As mentioned in the first chapter, the president is in actuality the high priest of the modern national religion, and thus he must conduct himself in such a way as to represent all the people, religiously as well as politically. He is required by law to proclaim a National Day of Prayer, and he is called upon to lead the nation in worship at moments of public trial or triumph and in mourning at the passing of the country's heroes. He is constantly asked to speak at or send congratulatory messages to religious conferences and ecclesiastical assemblies. According to Eisenhower's religious adviser, the Reverend Frederic E. Fox, the president is:

"Honorary Chairman" of many of our national charities. He is expected to bless almost all of America's voluntary groups—civic, business, and cultural. . . . While in the White House I also corresponded—over the President's signature or on his behalf—with thousands of individual citizens who were sick, bereaved, or ridden with fears and anxieties.[49]

The sacerdotal role of the president seemed to evolve naturally with the civil religion consensus. Eisenhower, who in 1956 appointed Congregationalist minister Fox as his staff person for religious affairs, was the first chief executive who created a structure to regularize the function. Unfortunately, in the twentieth century the presidency began taking on the character of a "sacred office," and by the time of Richard Nixon had even become, according to the editor of the *Christian Century*, "the ultimate deity in our nation-worship." This helps to explain why there was such an outpouring of grief over the assassination of President John F. Kennedy—many felt they had been personally violated. Because of the sacrosanct quality of the presidential office, it was difficult for large numbers of people to accept the inevitable verdict of the Watergate drama.[50] But when the tapes allowed Americans to enter directly into the Oval Office and there to encounter the rankest sort of political chicanery, the torrential outpouring of profanities and vulgarities, and the realization that the spiritual leader of the nation had lied and obstructed justice, Nixon lost the religious-mythic basis for popular support. With the shattering of the sacred aura that helped to sustain his power, the moral outrage of the American public insured that his fall would be all the more rapid and precipitous.[51]

Kennedy's narrow victory in 1960 was further evidence

that the civil religion consensus had supplanted the earlier Protestant one. As his close associate Theodore (Ted) Sorenson points out, the president was an active Roman Catholic who regularly attended Mass, yet he showed no awe of the hierarchy and had no reservations about the wisdom of separating church and state. He did not require or give preference to Catholics on his staff and was unconcerned about their religious beliefs. According to Sorenson, Kennedy "cared not a whit for theology" and never in his eleven-year association with him did he "disclose his personal views on man's relation to God."[52]

The Civil Faith Challenged   But the peaceful unfolding of the civil faith did not continue in the 1960s. Instead, crisis after crisis rocked the country and tore at the national fiber, setting brother against brother in a fearsome trial by ordeal that brought America's existence to the brink of disintegration and called into question the validity of the United States as most people knew it. What happened to civil religion in this third and perhaps greatest crisis in American history?

John Kennedy himself was wholeheartedly committed to civil religion, a fact that Robert Bellah underscores in his analysis of the martyred president's inaugural address. Implicit in the speech, Bellah argues, is the idea that political sovereignty rests with the people but the ultimate sovereignty belongs to God. The will of the people is not the criterion of right and wrong, but a higher standard exists that may judge the popular will as well as the president, if either is wrong. The rights of man are derived not from the generosity of the state—whether it is an expression of the will of an aristocratic monarch or of the people themselves—but from a higher source. Thus, the revolutionary significance of America lies in the idea that rights are ultimate in origin and the political structure may be radically altered if these rights are denied. Kennedy also implied a transcendent goal for the political process: "Here on earth God's work must truly be our own." Americans have the obligation to carry out God's will on earth by struggling against man's age-old enemies—tyranny, poverty, disease and war.[53]

Bellah goes on to raise a crucial question about civil religion itself. In the American version there is no formal creed and the concept of God is undefined. But what if an agnostic were elected President? Could this person use the word *God* in the same way Kennedy, Eisenhower and other presidents have?[54] Even though it was not articulated very precisely, this theological problem lay at the center of the school prayer controversy, the first great crisis which confronted American civil religion in the 1960s.

During the twentieth century the courts clearly have affirmed the principle of religious freedom and church-state separation. In the celebrated "Flag Salute case," Supreme Court Justice Robert H. Jackson served notice that "if there is any fixed star in our constitutional constellation, it is that no official, high or petty, can prescribe what shall be orthodox in politics, nationalism, religion, or other matters of opinion or force citizens to confess by word or act their faith therein."[55] High court decisions in 1947 and 1948 stressed that an impregnable wall existed between church and state and that public schools must be neutral in matters of religion. Most church leaders went along with this, but the next series of rulings stirred the ire of Protestants and Catholics alike. In the "Regent's Prayer case" (1962), the court forbade a school from prescribing a prayer, no matter how innocuous or inoffensive, for use by students. In the two "Bible Reading cases" (1963), schools were enjoined from requiring the devotional reading of a Bible passage, even without comment, in the classroom.[56]

The outpouring of wrath on the part of Christians surprised many observers, since the high tribunal had taken great pains to clarify that these decisions were designed to uphold individual rights, not to abolish religion from American life. President Kennedy forthrightly defended the court's action in a press conference:

We have in this case a very easy remedy, and that is to pray ourselves. And I would think that it would be a welcome reminder to every American family that we can pray a good deal more at home, we can attend our churches with a good deal more fidelity, and we can make the true meaning of prayer much more important in the lives of all of our children.[57]

However, many felt, as Representative Frank J. Becker of New York put it, that a "fraternity of secularists" was trying its best to restrict the free functioning of religious Americans. Billy Graham spoke out in a *Saturday Evening Post* article under the rubric of the "Voice of Dissent": "There is a movement gathering momentum in America to take the traditional concept of God out of our national life . . . to remove faith in God from the public conscience." Because militant, atheistic communism is "threatening to bury us," the people must re-examine the national goals and destiny, since an "American atheist administering a public office has essentially conceded the battle to communism."[58]

South Carolina Senator Strom Thurmond seconded the evangelist's remarks, affirming that "unless grassroots America rises up and demands that God be continued in a prominent place in our national lives," this country will "forfeit its opportunity for victory or even survival." The challenge posed by "the forces of secularism, those who would take God out of our national life and turn our country into a socialist America," is one of the "most crucial that any people ever faced."[59] Catholic Bishop Fulton Sheen declared that the Supreme Court ruling in effect said, "Thou shalt not pray" and it logically follows that atheists rather than God-fearing men will in the future be given the right to propaganda, while antiprayer and antireligion in schools will have the support of law. He labeled it "the death sentence upon our great country."[60] Similar sentiments were echoed by other political and religious leaders around the nation.

Congressman Becker's solution was the Prayer Amendment which for Christians became a most vexing issue. It simply stated that nothing in the Constitution would "prohibit the offering, reading from, or listening to prayers or biblical scripture, if participation therein is on a voluntary basis, in any governmental or public institution or place." Further, nothing would forbid "making reference to belief in, reliance upon, or invoking the aid of God or a Supreme Being in any governmental or public document, proceeding, activity, ceremony, school, institution, or place, or upon coinage, currency, or obligation of the United States."[61]

Although at first glance the amendment seemed innocuous, some Christians expressed serious reservations about it. Who or what authority would determine the content of the prayers and Bible readings? Did this endanger the constitutional separation of church and state? Would such actions compromise the integrity of genuine religion by setting up an officially sanctioned public cult marked by a lack of interior devotion and an abundance of national piety and thereby undermine the voluntarist, free church tradition of American Christianity? Would this threaten the consciences of minority religious groups by forcing them to conform to majority opinions? Becker was unable to secure passage of his measure, but similar proposals have been discussed in Washington from time to time and many evangelicals still hope for the adoption of a prayer amendment.

The Vietnam War   Obviously the prayer decisions constituted a threat to the civil religion consensus as they sharply divided religious people, but even more so did the Vietnam imbroglio. Nothing since the Civil War so separated Americans as this conflict. Faith in the country and national traditions was corroded, and on all sides sundry voices proclaimed the country's demise. According to Richard J. Neuhaus, even those who put their fingers on the genuine defects in American society seemed more interested in "humiliating and destroying the American reality than . . . healing and reconstituting that reality."[62]

As American forces became mired in a purposeless war, a mood of despair settled over the land and violence raged virtually unchecked in the cities and on the campuses, spawned by the example of that foreign conflict which played nightly on the television newscasts. The sense of patriotism and love of country which ordinarily had motivated Americans became the special province of that un-young, un-black, un-poor segment of the nation which Vice President Spiro T. Agnew crudely labeled "Middle America," and even a noteworthy portion of that group gave up hope for the country. As social critic Paul Goodman so poignantly put it: "Our case is astounding. For the first time in recorded history, the mention of country, community, place has lost its power to animate. Nobody but a scoundrel even tries it."[63]

Among the loudest voices prophesying national doom were those of evangelical Christians. Billy Graham, for example, said on "The Hour of Decision":

There is a hopelessness and a pessimism in the air not felt by any previous generation. We are like a convict condemned to death who is given his choice of food and drink before he walks the last mile. . . . We are the living dead, who walk but have little goal or destination.

In another radio sermon he drew a parallel between the Roman Empire immediately before its collapse and modern America:

In a decadent society the will to believe, to resist, to contend, to fight, to struggle, is gone. In place of this will to resist there is the desire to conform, to drift, to follow, to yield, and to give up. This is what happened to Rome, but it also applies to us. The same conditions that prevailed in Rome prevail in our society.[64]

Some invoked civil religion to generate support for the war, the popularity of which was steadily declining. Former President Eisenhower spoke out in the country's most widely read magazine, *Reader's Digest*, to condemn the lack of courage, loyalty and patriotism in the land, and to suggest that if this kind of discord had existed during World War 2 the United States would have lost. According to Eisenhower,

Americans were fighting in Vietnam as they had in the Second World War, "for our own salvation, for a way of life . . . to defend ourselves and other free nations against the eventual domination of communism." In his opinion, "it would be grossly immoral *not* to resist a tyranny whose openly avowed purpose is to subjugate the earth," and he demanded that the "illegal actions" of war protesters be stopped at once, because their activity was not honorable dissent but "rebellion, and it verges on treason." He expressed his "abiding faith in the good sense of the great majority of the American people," and called it "unthinkable that the voices of defeat" would be permitted to triumph in the land.[65]

Although Billy Graham was somewhat more cautious in his assessment of the conflict, he also endorsed it at a press conference in Denver, declaring that "the world is involved in a battle with communism. The President and most members of Congress are well united in their determination to stay in Viet Nam." He went on to say, "We are dealing with naked aggression," and "communism has to be stopped somewhere, whether it is in Hawaii or on the West Coast. The President believes it should be stopped in Viet Nam."[66] Fortunately, Graham did not look upon the struggle as an out-and-out holy war. For example, he did not go as far as Francis Cardinal Spellman who told the troops in Vietnam that "war has brought out the noblest instincts and the best traits of human courage in the annals of history," and that they were the "defense, protection, and salvation, not only of our country but . . . of civilization itself." The cardinal proclaimed that for the United States anything "less than victory is inconceivable."[67]

When Senator Mark Hatfield of Oregon at the National Prayer Breakfast on February 1, 1973, called for individual and corporate repentance "from the sin that scarred our national soul" and asked those present to be "Christ's messengers of reconciliation and peace" so they "can soothe the wounds of war, and renew the face of the earth and all mankind," he was operating within the civil religion tradition to criticize the collective national spirit of self-righteousness as epitomized by the war. Yet, the role of the civil faith was interpreted rather differently by fellow evangelical Billy Graham, a Nixon loyalist, who suggested Hatfield should have commended the president for his determination to obtain a cease-fire in Vietnam, instead of airing "political views and differences." According to Graham "this would have had a unifying effect that the Country desperately needs at this time."[68] This disagreement between two leading evangelicals illustrates poignantly how the dilemma of the most frustrating conflict in American history spilled over into the realm of civil religion.

Richard Nixon and Watergate   President Lyndon B. Johnson, who guided the nation's destiny during much of the Vietnam struggle, was an enigma to evangelicals in particular. His coarse, even vulgar demeanor hardly endeared him to serious Christians, yet he was on intimate terms with Billy Graham and the evangelist regarded the president as a man of sincere faith. In fact Johnson asked Graham to deliver the sermon at an interfaith worship service in Washington's National City Christian Church on the morning of the inauguration in 1965, and he was a frequent guest at the White House.[69] But Johnson's inability to end the Vietnam conflict discredited him in the eyes of the public, and Richard Nixon appeared on the scene as the knight in shining armor who would lead the nation out of the quagmire of Southeast Asia. Reared as a Quaker in California, Nixon was a person whose religious feelings seemed to run deep. But what came out of his administration was the most shattering blow of all to modern American civil religion.

For all intents the inaugural in 1969 was a festival of civil worship. Prayers were offered by representatives of the four major faiths, Graham delivered an invocation which was more of a sermon than a prayer and the presidential address contained references to God, the Bible, spirit, American virtues and vices, and faith in the nation's future. Nixon suggested that the country was torn by "a crisis of the spirit" and for this it needed "an answer of the spirit."[70]

Like Eisenhower, President Nixon manifested a highly visible public faith. He sponsored private, by invitation only, religious services in the East Room of the White House, and speakers at these gatherings represented a wide spectrum of theological opinion (except the far left and right). But these guest clergy never engaged in anything that might pass for genuinely prophetic preaching.[71] Although the president's own motives for holding these irregularly scheduled worship services are not altogether clear, two of his aides admitted later that they utilized invitations to them for "stroking," that is, appeasing and rewarding friends or fulfilling social obligations to people.[72]

Like his predecessors, President Nixon addressed ecclesiastical assemblies, hosted delegations and issued the usual official prayers and proclamations of a religious character. In addition he appeared to enjoy the company of prominent church leaders like Norman Vincent Peale, Billy Graham and Terence Cardinal Cooke. In 1971 Religious Heritage of America, whose outgoing head W. Clement Stone was a Nixon admirer, named the U.S. president "Churchman of the Year" for "carrying his deep religious commitment into the Presidency."[73]

The chief executive's relationship with Graham is especially intriguing. They had been friends since Nixon's senatorial days; Graham supported him for president in 1960 and he seems to have had a part in Nixon's decision to run in 1968. The president made celebrated appearances at the evangelist's East Tennessee Crusade in 1970 and the Billy Graham Day observance in Charlotte, North Carolina in 1971, while Graham often visited the White House and preached at more Nixon services there than anyone else. In 1972 the evangelist endorsed Nixon for re-election, and stood by his friend virtually to the bitter end of the Watergate tragedy.[74]

Nixon presented a peculiar problem to evangelical Protestants. Because the president was essentially the high priest of the civil religion and most rank-and-file Christians were unaware of the extent to which the civil faith had become devoid of genuine spiritual content, evangelicals were concerned that he be a committed Christian. Thus, they often tended to misinterpret presidential expressions of religiosity as professions of faith in Christ. For obvious reasons evangelicals did not identify closely with Kennedy or Johnson, but in Nixon many believed they had found "one of our own."[75] This partly explains why so many of them enthusiastically backed him for a second term in 1972. Moreover, accounts of religious activity in Washington in the latter half of the seventies indicate that many believers continue to manifest a penchant to identify with somewhat superficial signals of evangelical faith by public officials.[76]

Nixon's outward religiosity, however, did not fool everyone in the evangelical community. For example, Carl F. H. Henry, the former editor of *Christianity Today*, describing an interview he had with the Republican candidate in 1968, commented that Nixon "was remarkably imprecise about spiritual realities and enduring ethical concerns," and that he was "the confident champion of a free world where divine Providence benevolently guarantees America's ongoing global leadership rather than, as in the Bill of Rights, towers as supreme Source, Sanction, and Stipulator of universal human rights." Then, too, during the 1972 election campaign a spirited group organized an "Evangelicals for McGovern" committee to call attention to what they strongly felt were Nixon's moral deficiencies and to raise funds for his Democratic opponent.[77]

Needless to say, Nixon did not hesitate to utilize civil religion to rally support for his policies. In the 1970 State of the Union message he asked God to give wisdom, strength and idealism so that "America can fulfill its destiny of being the world's best hope" for liberty, opportunity, progress and peace for all people.[78] In the Second Inaugural Address, Nixon asked his listeners "to renew faith in ourselves and

America" as they faced the challenges of the future. He requested prayers for "God's help in making decisions that are right for America" and urged people to "go forward from here confident in hope, strong in our faith in one another, sustained by our faith in God who created us, and strong always to serve His purposes."[79] In all fairness it must not be forgotten that Senator McGovern also drew upon civil religion rhetoric in his presidential campaign, most notably in his Wheaton College speech of October 11, 1972.

As the Watergate scandal revealed, Nixon not only lacked sincerity in his religious affirmations but also was actually exploiting the evangelicals. A cogent example was the Honor America Day rally in Washington on July 4, 1970. The idea for it arose out of a conversation between Nixon and Graham in which the latter said: "Mr. President, everyone talks about what's wrong with America. Why doesn't someone talk about what's *right* with America?" Thereupon Graham, comedian Bob Hope, Hobart Lewis of the *Reader's Digest* and hotel magnate J. Willard Marriott organized a celebration in which ordinary citizens could speak out for the country. The White House assigned Jeb Magruder as the "liaison person" to make sure "the event was run the way Haldeman and the President wanted it run." For most individuals it was merely a patriotic Fourth of July ceremony, featuring Graham as the preacher in a morning religious service and big-name entertainment in the evening. However, Magruder points out in his memoirs that for the White House clique it "was a political event, one in which honoring America was closely intertwined with supporting Richard Nixon, and in particular with supporting his policy in Vietnam at a time when a great many people were opposing it with rallies of their own." Nixon's lieutenants stage-managed the whole affair and regarded it as a success.[80]

The unfolding drama of Watergate—from the break-in, cover-up, dirty tricks, wiretapping, burglaries, lying, profanity and character assassination to the other sordid events of this tragic moment in American history—raised questions of profound moral and spiritual significance. Nixon's endeavor to sidestep them by appealing to civil religion fell totally flat. At the National Prayer Breakfast on January 31, 1974, the president declared: "Too often we are a little too arrogant. We try to talk and tell Him what we want. What all of us need to do, and what this nation needs to do, is to pray in silence and listen to God to find out what He wants us to do." Then he proceeded to expound on the prayer life of Lincoln. The Reverend John Huffman insightfully gauged the temper of Nixon's comments when he remarked to a newspaper reporter: "To exegete the writings and prayer life of a previous president instead of the Bible is to make the history of the nation the divine authority, not God. This is Baalism."[81]

With the release of the taped conversations in the Oval Office, Nixon's doom was sealed. Before Congress could impeach him, on August 9, 1974 he turned over the reins to Vice President Gerald Ford and stepped down. This event, too, drew heavily upon the resources of civil religion. In a presidential system the chief of state and head of government are the same and power is personalized in the chief executive and, as Michael Novak perceptively comments, the force of the civil religion helped to drive Nixon from the White House because the very office itself, not the particular individual occupying it at the time, carried "the sacred seal" and "the public outrage confirmed the sanctity of the office."[82] Further, Nixon's resignation and subsequent disappearance from the public scene took on the character of a ritual of national cleansing and atonement that strengthened the resolve of people to live and function more circumspectly within the boundaries of the law. The mass media portrayed it as a great national tragedy and Americans shared in the grief and suffering of the fallen president and his family. Also, the televised Watergate hearings, public confessions of misdeeds and trials of the principals provided the opportunity for a sort of national catharsis.[83] Thus, it can be argued that civil religion provided support for the needed changes which many hoped would prevent another Watergate from occurring in the future.

It logically followed that the new president would wrap himself in the cloak of the civil religion. On his first day in office Ford asked the American people to confirm him "with your prayers" and solemnly promised "to do what is right as God gives me to see the right."[84] Pardoning his predecessor only a month later, President Ford declared that he had sought God's guidance and searched his "own conscience with special diligence to determine the right thing to do." He affirmed his belief that "I, not as President, but as a humble servant of God will receive justice without mercy if I fail to show mercy."[85] In the same manner as other presidents, his speeches were liberally sprinkled with references to God and prayer, and he delivered messages at such significant religious functions as the National Prayer Breakfasts, the National Association of Evangelicals convention in February 1976 and the International Eucharistic Congress in August 1976.

It seems fair to conclude that the Watergate imbroglio had exposed the Nixon presidency for what it really was—an unscrupulous grasp for personal power. But even worse, it had become a form of idolatry. The president was the priest of the American civil religion and the well-being of the nation was identified with his welfare and survival. Whatever was necessary to keep him in power was automatically justifiable. Illegal actions, regardless of their nature, if they were performed in the name of national security, were morally acceptable. The failure of the attempt to conceal these illicit deeds illustrates the validity of the hallowed doctrine that divine judgment on unjust policies and evil institutions can be expected. If America was to be "one nation under God," then the deification of the nation and its security had to be exorcised from the land and the false high priest expelled from the White House. National meaning would have to be found elsewhere than at the seat of political power and in the blind alley of national interests as interpreted by the high priest of the civil religion.

This is the dilemma which the civil religion now faces. No state or person possesses ultimate power—only the Creator and Sustainer of all things may lay claim to that. Yet, the public faith seems to be a vital element of the national fabric, and it is unrealistic to expect it to disappear from the United States in the near future. But the question remains—is civil religion beneficial to the healthy functioning of the public order, or does it interfere with God's purposes for the national community? Does civil religion usurp the prerogatives of Jesus Christ or can it coexist in modern American society in a positive way with a virile evangelical faith? The next two chapters will be addressed to this issue.

4
CIVIL RELIGION AS A COMMON FAITH FOR THE COMMON GOOD

Congressman John B. Anderson writes in *Vision and Betrayal in America* that there is a need to rediscover and rearticulate American civil religion. He maintains that every nation has a "civil religion," a body of national ideology and traditions that provides the glue to hold in place the diverse religious, ethnic and regional interests of the country. No civil society can exist without such a religion, and the problem facing Americans is to insure that their civic faith is a positive one, to see that it stands for what is right and noblest in man's capacities.[1]

Many Americans feel that the bonds of loyalty that hold their national community together are dissolving, and they would agree that Anderson's plea merits serious consideration. From a historical standpoint, a nation exists when a people feels and wills that they have something in common and they are committed to a collective destiny on earth.[2] But in the United States this sense of commonality and consciousness of national identity and purpose seems to be in jeopardy. During the previous century most Americans saw their country as the bearer of transcendent norms, a new order for the ages, set apart by divine Providence for a mission of world redemption, while now the traditional religious consensus is under fire. The symbols of loyalty and national reverence apparently are in a state of decay and disuse, as national holidays have been transformed into long weekends, and conservative law-and-order people and racists have taken possession of the flag. Some speculate whether the "new ethnicity" and the endeavor to rewrite history to include all the various groups which have been left out may have mortally wounded the concept of one homogeneous American people and the sense of nationality emanating from this.

Although social and racial tensions are tearing at the national fabric, a stultifying sense of indifference has settled over the land, and more and more people look only to securing their own personal well-being. Many have abandoned hope of a better future in the face of declining American world power, persistent economic troubles, the energy crisis and the threat of environmental destruction. In short, the United States stands in great need of a public sense of purpose and commitment, and the question of what contribution the common faith can make is of vital concern to people who believe American society is worth preserving. What follows in this chapter is a presentation of the views expounded by those who find meaningful answers in civil religion.

A Transcendent or a Statist Religion?   Two noted exponents of the concept, Robert N. Bellah and Sidney E. Mead, stress that the civil faith is transcendent and stands in judgment over the state and its officials. Sociologist Bellah points out that in American political theory sovereignty rests "with the people, but implicitly, and often explicitly, the ultimate sovereignty has been attributed to God." Not the will of the people but a higher power is the criterion of right and wrong, and so civil religion is not the worship of the nation but rather "an understanding of the American experience in the light of ultimate and universal reality."[3] Historian Mead calls attention to the problem of religious sectarianism. He suggests that the "neutral" civil authority promotes pluralism, in order to keep any one sect from monopolizing the "definition of truth" and imposing this on the others and to use the sects to communicate to their members the universal verity of God's primacy over all human institutions. This, he argues, is diametrically opposite to the worship of the nation, state or "American way of life." The civil authority stands above religious groups and adjudicates their differences when these threaten to disrupt the public order. Thus, the primary religious concern in America must be to guard against national idolatry, the temptation for the state to become God. When the nation assumes the garb of the church, it will attempt to subject other peoples and nations to its law and will.[4]

Theologian John E. Smylie contends that in the late nineteenth century the American nation, in fact, came to be endowed with churchly attributes. It now functions "as the primary agent of God's meaningful activity in history," is the "primary society in terms of which individual Americans discovered personal and group identity," and is "the community of righteousness." In effect the national community became the agency of sanctification.[5] In this new role, however, it only replaces the churches and, like the ecclesiastical bodies, the nation is subject to a higher authority. With the demise of the Protestant consensus, civil religion had to assume the burden of providing society with moral values, a task which was carried out through the medium of the public schools.

A healthy civil religion affords a bulwark against deification of the state. The concept of "this nation under God" means that the state is not the Almighty and it does not compete with him for the allegiance and worship which belong to him alone. As evangelical political scientist Perry C. Cotham stresses, the phrase is an acknowledgment that "*all* political communities, systems, and policies are under the judgment and mercy of God."[6] It implies the impossibility of enlisting the support of the Supreme Being for national endeavors and that the nation is subject to God's chastisement for its shortcomings. Such a civil faith forbids the state to usurp the place of God and denies it the power to be the final arbiter of morality. As Bellah emphasizes, this is not idolatrous national self-worship but "the subordination of the nation to ethical principles that transcend it and in terms of which it should be judged."[7]

This stance is illustrated by an excerpt from the Bicentennial Fourth of July sermon of the Reverend George S. Knieriemen, Jr., pastor of the North Como Presbyterian Church in St. Paul, Minnesota:

There are two flags here in our church this morning—as there always are. One represents our nation. The other represents the Christian Church. They stand on the same level and appear to be equal. Both stand off to the side, not in the center. The center is reserved for the cross. Both flags stand under it—for it represents the God we know best because of the love of Christ. The American flag, like the nation, stands under God. The allegiance we give to it is of a different and lesser order than the allegiance we give our Lord. Otherwise, the words "this nation under God" do not, for us, mean what they say.[8]

Thus, civil religion is the only major opening to transcendence for most Americans, and it constitutes the unifying element in society that can lift people above sectarian strife. Because the national community is above all a spiritual entity, comprised of people sharing a body of convictions that set them apart from other such groups, it automatically possesses some sort of symbol system—a civil faith—to guide it.[9] This promotes a sense of corporate identity, provides an acceptable set of beliefs about the nation's origins, its place before God and its historical destiny, and fleshes out the common core of ideas and values. In this manner religion assumes the function of providing support for the performance of civic duties and enables people voluntarily to live up to the requirements of citizenship.

Civil religion in America, as Neal Riemer cogently suggests, civilizes "the savage beast of state." It validates the state's powers and legitimizes its authority by establishing, "under God," the rules of the game. These regulations determine the high purposes of civil society and the state (the more perfect union, justice, domestic tranquility, the common defense, the general welfare, the blessings of liberty). Also, these rules spell out the legitimate authority of government and rights of citizens and clarify the processes and spirit that will characterize the conduct of public affairs.[10] Lutheran radio minister Oswald Hoffmann adds: "Any government that does not recognize its responsibility under God has lost one legitimate claim, probably the most important one of all, to legitimate authority."[11] This means that civil religion is the foundation of the constitutional order and civic freedom and contributes immeasurably to the stability of the American system.

Exponents of a transcendent civil religion suggest that it is unlikely that liberal democracy can survive without this framework. The preservation of American rights hinges upon the realization that they are more than manmade; they emanate from the hands of "nature's God." Not only did the Founding Fathers possess extraordinary wisdom and insight, but they also were guided by Providence, and therefore Western democracy is not the product of the whims of human ingenuity but stems from divine sources.[12] In a time when the cause of political liberty has suffered defeat after defeat in all parts of the world and the number of nations which uphold the ideals of democracy and human rights is steadily declining, Americans need to look to the transcendent source of their freedom instead of simply trusting in armed might to hold back the forces of tyranny stalking the globe.

American Civil Religion and National Ideals   Mead reminds Americans that "the religion of the Republic is essentially prophetic," that is, "its ideals and aspirations stand in constant judgment over the passing shenanigans of the people, reminding them of the standards by which their current practices and those of their nation are ever being judged and found wanting."[13] Inherent in the American way of life is a process of constant self-evaluation. There are rights which must not be violated, procedures for defending those rights and transcendent ideals that hold national practices accountable at any given historical moment. Michael Novak intimates that "civil religion legitimizes, even necessitates, incessant criticism" of the American way of life. "Self-criticism and self-transcendence" are a vital aspect of the American system.[14]

Thus, the civil faith provides a view of God in his relationship to all nations and calls attention to his demands for social justice. It has served both as an impetus for Americans to include increasing numbers of people within the scope of national concern and as a source of inspiration for reformers throughout the nation's history. They have pointed to the stated ideals of America and the great documents of its history and applied them as measuring rods to call attention to shortcomings. When confronted with evil the American ritual response has not been indifference or resignation but: "What can we *do* about it?" A desire for corrective action is one of the most distinctive characteristics of the American people. Theologian and church historian Martin E. Marty labels this the "prophetic" mode of civil religion, as contrasted to its "priestly" form which is dealt with in the next chapter, and he argues that a nation "under" a transcendent God is both shaped and judged by this Deity.[15]

A noteworthy example of how the resources of civil religion have been used to summon the nation to fulfill its ideals and responsibilities is the National Day for Humiliation, Fasting, and Prayer. On December 20, 1973 Mark Hatfield introduced a joint resolution in the Senate (modeled closely after one written by Abraham Lincoln) which provided for setting aside April 30, 1974 as a day of national repentance. The Oregon solon referred to the erosion of trust in leaders in all parts of life, the wasteful misuse of the world's natural resources, the divisions tearing the country apart and the lack of a spiritual foundation on which to restore the nation's vision and purpose. Americans had grown comfortable in their self-righteousness, but this led only to greater peril because of materialism, social injustice and excessive concern with armed force. Hatfield expressed his "firm conviction that a genuine spirit of repentance, infecting the climate of our Nation at all levels, can heal the wounds that presently afflict us," and national repentance would produce authentic renewal and transformation.[16] The resolution was unanimously passed by the Senate and forwarded to the House of Representatives.

The carefully worded statement invoked civil religion in a sensitive but incisive manner as it focused attention on national transgressions and called the American people to repentance. Although the resolution was misunderstood by some who regarded it simply as contentless religiosity and misused by others to back up their own conservative rejection of modern trends and social change, an analysis of it reveals the creative possibilities latent in the civil faith. The preamble affirmed that nations and men alike "owe their dependence upon the overruling power of God" and it is their duty to confess their sins and transgressions and seek divine mercy and pardon. The sins delineated were genuinely national ones—abuse of God's bounties bestowed upon the American people and the assumption that these blessings were the result of their superior wisdom and virtue; an intoxication with "unbroken success" that has instilled a feeling of self-sufficiency; an obsession with national security; a failure "to respond, personally and collectively, with sacrifice and uncompromised commitment to the unmet needs of their fellow man, both at home and abroad"; and an absorption "with the selfish pursuits of pleasure and profit" that has "blinded ourselves to God's standard of justice and righteousness for this society." The Senate resolution itself called upon the American people to humble themselves before the Creator, acknowledge their final dependence upon him and repent of national sins.[17]

In the end the House failed to act, and although no official congressional approval of the measure was reached by April 30, large numbers of Americans still observed the special day. Thirty-three state governors and dozens of mayors issued proclamations recognizing it, thousands of churches were open for prayer vigils, and Protestant, Catholic and Orthodox leaders voiced their support. The involvement of evangelicals was especially visible, more so than traditional ecumenical figures because many of them were leery of possible conservative overtones in the observance. The Senate devoted the entire morning of April 30 to a discussion of the resolution, and here the implications of utilizing the civil religion to direct the nation back to its first principles were thoroughly examined.[18]

In an eloquent fashion Senator Harold Hughes of Iowa reviewed the manifestations of civil religion. He concluded that "if we believe God still concerns Himself in the affairs of men and nations, and if we believe in the morality that that Deity has set out for us to follow," then the vast majority of Americans will recognize the need for prayer, humiliation and seeking God's forgiveness. This is not a "political act" because to take such a thing lightly "would be a desecration against God." Rather, it is calling on God to honor his creation and "to intervene in the affairs of man that there might be justice, continued freedom, love, lack of hunger, clothing for the naked, and all the things we need in this expression of love for those with whom we have been brought to live together on this earth." Hughes expressed the hope that:

> We can today have a new beginning in justice, fairness, equality, care, and concern for our brothers and sisters on this Earth; and that as a nation our leaders can rid themselves of their pride and arrogance, that all of us can dare be humble and bow before God and say, "Forgive me, for I have sinned," and that in doing this our Father will hear, and redirect us, and reguide us as a nation, because He had a hand in selecting us for these positions of power.[19]

A not-so-subtle difference in perception of the divine demand upon America was expressed by Senator Carl Curtis of Nebraska. Although wholeheartedly endorsing the resolution, he insisted that it is not necessary to attempt to enumerate here or any place else "what might be termed our national sins." That is "a bit morbid," and besides the sovereign God knows all anyway. "It will not be necessary that we provide Him with a subscription to one or more of the daily papers published in the country for Him to know what our national sins are."[20]

Barry Goldwater was more blunt in his reaction to the measure. He objected to the reference to having made an idol out of the pursuit of national security and declared that "no nation in the history of man" has done as much as the United States to eliminate poverty, to stamp out starvation and to help people less fortunate. The Arizona senator maintained that "a spirit of humbleness and gratitude for the many blessings we have is one thing," but he could not agree with any suggestion "that we as a nation and people should feel humiliated." He summed up his position with the affirmation:

> Personally, I am so darn proud to be an American that I have no room to feel humiliated. I do not like some of the things that have been going on but they do not humiliate me. They are problems brought on by years of not paying attention to morals or ethics, so I will include in my prayers a prayer that all of us elected or nonelected pay attention to these two important facets of life.

Later on he reiterated that "we feel no humility in the fact that we are Americans" and he wanted it made clear "that when we talk of humiliation, I do not want someone in a godless country saying we are ashamed of our country."[21]

In response, Senator Lawton Chiles of Florida explained that the resolution did not call for people to be "ashamed of our country in any way" or to "humble ourselves before any other ideology or any other being." But Americans "have become so proud" as to reach the point "where we do not think that we can humble ourselves before God any more." Hughes agreed with Chiles and, revealing a deep sensitivity to the divine claim on the nation, confessed his belief that:

> If humiliating myself before God is a weakness, then I prefer to be weak. If asking for forgiveness and seeking repentance from the Almighty Creator is going to be embarrassing to me before other nations, then I prefer to be embarrassed.

In his opinion "there is no fear in expressing humiliation before God the Creator." Because many who do not acknowledge God simply assume that we take the position "God is on our side," the expression of humiliation is one way of demonstrating that no matter what we can do, we have not done enough to meet his demands.[22]

Thus, the sponsors of the National Day for Humiliation, Fasting, and Prayer utilized civil religion concepts to urge the nation to reaffirm its ideals. The country was falling short of its creative possibilities and needed to submit once more to the demands of the transcendent God. What they did not do was glorify America as God's chosen people or invoke his blessing upon the current policies of the regime and practices of its officials.

The Covenant Nation   A pervasive theme in American civil religion is that of covenant. As noted previously this can be traced back to the Puritans who perceived themselves as being on a divinely ordained errand into the wilderness of the New World where God would establish his kingdom of righteousness. John Winthrop expressed the idea that his colonists had entered into a covenant with God and that they would be a "city upon a hill" on which the eyes of all the world would be fixed. They had crossed the Red Sea of the Atlantic Ocean to make their homes in the promised land, and the new polity was built on the Old Testament notion of a covenant between God and the people who were collectively responsible for their actions.

John A. MacKay, theologian and former president of

Princeton Seminary, posits the notion that the covenant relation which constituted Israel's nationhood continues as a valid pattern for national groups today. Wherever and whenever Christians found themselves in a situation where they were obliged to exercise political responsibility, the Old Testament theocratic concept centering in the covenant between God and Israel took on contemporary significance. MacKay argues that nations fall into three classes according to their attitudes toward the divine: the *secular nation* eliminates God from all official connection with its life and culture and declares that its supreme loyalty is to ideology; the *demonic nation* transforms itself into an ultimate, taking the place of God, or deifies some reality associated with national life; the *covenant nation* recognizes its dependence upon God and responsibility to him. Examples of these three types are modern France, Nazi Germany and the United States respectively.

Because America as a covenant nation regards God as the source of human rights and recognizes that liberty is from him, the basis of its democracy is nothing less than theocracy. However, the covenant does not imply that America is the favorite of the Deity or that God is Americanized, but rather, that his purposes stand above the nation and its interests, and the highest role a nation can play is to reflect God's righteousness in national policy and all of life's relationships. This obligates America to share its natural bounties with other peoples on a world scale. The American people have covenanted with God who, "while being the God of all people, becomes in a very special sense the God of all those who accept His purpose for human life." If the United States remains loyal to its spiritual heritage, it will not pass away as a nation.[23]

In a decidedly different fashion, Bellah in *The Broken Covenant* also advances the thesis that the covenant myth contributed vitally to the development of the American moral fiber, but he points out that a growing emphasis on personal gratification and the decline of belief in all forms of obligation—to one's occupation, family and country—is eroding the moral base of society.[24] In each of the last three centuries America has gone through times of trial that called into question the very existence of the nation. The first was the struggle for independence and the institution of liberty. The second was the confrontation over the issue of slavery and whether the Union could be preserved and the equal protection of the laws extended to all members of society. The third time of testing is the twentieth-century crisis of national meaning, of justice and order at home and in the world and of how America can engage in responsible action in a revolutionary world.[25]

Bellah contends that America was founded upon the Puritan covenant pattern which in the eighteenth century converged with the republican ideal flowing from the Enlightenment. Both patterns saw society based upon the deep inner commitment of its members—the former through conversion and the latter through republican virtue. The Declaration of Independence with its appeal to the "laws of nature and nature's God" and the mutual "pledge to each other" of "our lives, our fortunes, and our sacred honor" fused the ultimate legitimating principles of both traditions and reflected the republican formula of a civil compact and the Puritan formula of the covenant. However, the covenant ideal with its concern for the common cause was challenged by another view, the utilitarian, which emphasized individual self-interest. The liberation of the revolution had to move toward the creation of new structures or the gains would have been lost. The problem was resolved by the drafting of the Constitution, a structure of liberty which established the future in the form of a new covenant.

Bellah believes that Americans failed their covenant almost before it had been made, because they founded their new commonwealth on a double crime—the dispossession of the Indians and enslavement of Africans. The ambiguity latent in the conception of being a chosen nation kept Americans from a full awareness of the magnitude of their misdeeds. However, the myths of civil religion challenged them to renew their covenantal vows and this finally brought the issue to a head in the crisis over slavery. National aggrandizement also slipped out of the covenant's control and became imperialism, while an analogous development took place on the personal level in the form of aggressive dominance over others—the gospel of wealth and the cult of success. At the same time, the economic system of modern industrialism and corporate capitalism undermined the fundamental American ideology of economic independence as the basis of the political order. Today, the doctrine that happiness is to be attained through limitless material acquisition dominates national thinking, while poverty and its attendant evils continue to afflict a significant portion of the populace.

Bellah warns Americans to recognize the reality that the covenant has been broken and current civil religion is an empty shell. He claims that the solution to this present problem is to transform the shattered external covenant into an internal one. In the past, religious and ethical revivals filled the covenant with meaning, and this must take place today if America is to survive its third and greatest crisis. People must not simply try to reclaim the past but to view it critically and utilize tradition as a stimulus to national regeneration. He urges the reaffirmation of the external covenant and the civil religion and the full implementation of the ideals contained in the fundamental documents of the nation. But America also needs a rebirth of imaginative vision that will infuse the covenant with positive meaning and provide an enduring religious and moral foundation for the nation in the future.

Although he rejects Bellah's formulation of civil religion and shies away from the concept as much as possible, Lutheran theologian Richard J. Neuhaus in his provocative work, *Time Toward Home*, places great emphasis on the theme of covenant and the vision of a future when God will finish that which he has started.[26] The covenant has Americans making promises to Another, ones that are in response to his prior promise to bring history—the whole of reality—to completion. Their experience is an important part of a history, the fulfillment of which is assured. The existence of the American covenant, however, is not specifically revealed by God but is derivative from the more generally revealed divine intentions in history. Acceptance of the covenant notion requires that Christians in particular share in the American experience and accept responsibility for playing an active role in its redemption.

Belief in the covenant, Neuhaus contends, does not lead to arrogance but to humility because it means the nation is accountable to judgment by the Almighty. It also can restore the faith in the future which so many modern people have abandoned. Thus, "covenant thinking envisions America as a lively experiment with promises to keep and a destiny to be realized within universal history," but at the same time the conditional character of this existence serves as a check on hubris.[27] Moreover, the covenant provides the country with a sound base for patriotism, one that "is modest in the knowledge that America is under judgment, and confident in the hope that America may yet be a blessing and not a curse to the nations of the earth."[28]

In other words, the idea of covenant imposes upon the United States an awesome burden of responsibility. It stands as a humane, liberating example for other peoples and demonstrates the benefits of freedom and self-government under God. The goal of international justice is set before this nation, and it possesses the spiritual and material resources to lead the world in that direction. As Methodist theologian Merrill R. Abbey forcefully puts it, the covenant has provided "the springs of vitality" for American life. From it comes not "gentle persuasion and optional responses" but the "imperatives" to secure the fulfillment of the American dream for those citizens now excluded from it and to render assistance to the less fortunate peoples of the world. Congressman John Anderson agrees wholeheartedly with this, adding that a challenge has been presented to Americans really to "make this great country of ours, with all of its great potential for good . . . a city upon a hill!"[29]

The Practical Application of Civil Religion   Bellah argues persuasively that before 1861 abolitionists like William Lloyd Garrison and Theodore Weld used the symbols and rhetoric of civil religion with considerable effectiveness to whip up opposition to slavery.[30] Much more significant are the well-known actions of Lincoln in the struggle to preserve the Union which, according to popular Christian thinker Elton Trueblood, are "one of the brightest features of the civil religion of America." He delineates three basic ideas in Lincoln's civil theology: God has a purpose, finite men are to be the Almighty's instruments in the fulfillment of his purpose and the American people are called to a special vocation for the sake of the world.[31] In his 1863 Thanksgiving Day Proclamation, Gettysburg Address and Second Inaugural Address, Lincoln repeatedly invoked civil religion concepts in the quest for the restoration of national unity. In the last-named speech, as Bellah emphasizes, the president also related slavery and the war in an ultimate perspective:

If we shall suppose that American slavery is one of those offenses which, in the providence of God, must needs come, but which, having continued through His appointed time, He now wills to remove, and that He gives to both North and South this terrible war as the woe due to those by whom the offense came, shall we discern therein any departure from those divine attributes which the believers in a living God always ascribe to Him? Fondly do we hope, fervently do we pray, that this mighty scourge of war may speedily pass away. Yet, if God wills that it continue until all the wealth piled by the bondsman's two hundred and fifty years of unrequited toil shall be sunk, and until every drop of blood drawn with the lash shall be paid by another drawn with the sword, as was said three thousand years ago, so still it must be said "the judgements of the Lord are true and righteous altogether."

127

And then he closed on a note of reconciliation: "With malice toward none, with charity for all...."[32]

Lincoln's actions during the Civil War illustrate Bellah's contention that "the basis of our civil religion is the intent to subordinate politics to ethical principles that transcend it." These principles are that the nation exists under divine judgment and that it must meet basic moral commitments to all members of society for justice, equality and some kind of charity. The Great Emancipator was intuitively aware of the obligation to use the political process to achieve the transcendent goal of establishing equality and justice.[33]

A more contemporary example of the creative possibilities inherent in civil religion and how it can be used to secure positive gains in the political realm is the civil rights movement of the 1960s. Few today can forget how Dr. Martin Luther King, Jr. used religious imagery with such telling effect in his speeches and statements. Take, for instance, his "I Have a Dream" address at the August 28, 1963 march on Washington rally which is a landmark in American oratory. To the thousands assembled before the Lincoln Memorial and the millions watching on television King proclaimed the harsh reality that one hundred years after the Emancipation Proclamation the Negro still was not free, but was crippled by the manacles of segregation and chains of discrimination and living on a lonely island of poverty in a vast ocean of material prosperity. He asserted that there would be no rest or tranquility in America until blacks were granted full citizenship and "the bright day of justice emerges."

In spite of setbacks and frustrations, King held fast to a dream of a radically changed America where the creed "all men created equal" would be put into practice. In moving fashion he drew upon the words of the prophet Isaiah:

I have a dream that one day every valley shall be exalted, every hill and mountain shall be made low, the rough place will be made plain, and the crooked places will be made straight, and the glory of the Lord shall be revealed, and all flesh shall see it together.

King then told about his dream of a day "when all God's children will be able to sing with new meaning, 'My country 'tis of thee, sweet land of liberty, of thee I sing. Land where my fathers died, land of the Pilgrims' pride, from every mountainside, let freedom ring.' " To the deafening roar of the crowd, he finished his dream:

> When we let freedom ring, when we let it ring from every village and every hamlet, from every state and every city, we will be able to speed up that day when all God's children, black men and white men, Jews and Gentiles, Protestants and Catholics, will be able to join hands and sing in the words of the old Negro spiritual, "Free at last! Free at last! Thank God almighty, we are free at last!"[34]

King moved the conscience of America in a way few people have been able to do as he called for the implementation of equality and justice. But, the attainment of these goals required political action as well as moral commitment. Thus, both Presidents Kennedy and Johnson made use of civil religion symbols and phraseology in their appeals to Congress and the nation for the adoption of civil rights legislation and public acceptance of these measures. For instance, when Kennedy called up the Alabama National Guard to carry out the integration of the state university there, he explained his actions in a nationally televised address on June 11, 1963. He called the granting of full rights to blacks primarily a "moral issue," one that "is as old as the Scriptures and is as clear as the American Constitution." The president stressed that the nation "will not be truly free until all its citizens are free," and that America is facing "a moral crisis as a country and a people." It is time to act in Congress, state and local legislative bodies and "in all of our daily lives." Still, legislation "cannot solve this problem alone. It must be solved in the homes of every American in every community across our country."[35]

After his accession to the presidency, Johnson lent full support to the civil rights program of his predecessor and worked diligently to secure passage of the requisite measures. For example, addressing a Christian leadership seminar of the Southern Baptist Convention on March 25, 1964, the new president called upon those present to work for adoption of his civil rights proposals. He told the Baptists that "in more than three decades of public life, I have seen firsthand how basic spiritual beliefs and deeds can shatter barriers of politics and bigotry." He had seen them crumble in the presence of faith, and "from this experience I have drawn new hope that the seemingly insurmountable moral issues that we face at home and abroad today can be resolved by men of strong faith and men of brave deeds." He urged them not to let the doctrine of separation of church and state bring about a divorce of spiritual values from secular affairs and affirmed that "the identity of private morality and public conscience" is deeply rooted in the American tradition and Constitution. In such fashion he endeavored, successfully it might be added, to obtain the endorsement of this key bloc for his program.[36]

In the following year Johnson proposed a strong voting rights bill, and in a televised address to Congress on March 15 he utilized civil religion terminology to mobilize support for the attainment of what he considered a pressing national goal. "Rarely are we met with a challenge, not to our growth or abundance, our welfare or our security, but rather to the values and the purposes and the meaning of our beloved Nation," the president eloquently asserted. The matter of equal rights before the law for black Americans is such a question, and should we defeat every enemy, double our wealth, conquer the stars and "still be unequal to this issue, then we will have failed as a people and as a nation." He went on to say that the United States was the "first nation in the history of the world to be founded with a purpose," that is, every citizen is created equal and shares in human dignity. Arguing for the right of all to vote, he declared that "it is wrong—deadly wrong" to deny the franchise to any American.

Johnson pointed out that a century had passed since equality was promised to American blacks and it was still unkept. "The time of justice is now come. . . . It is right in the eyes of man and God that it should come. . . . Equality depends not on the force of arms or tear gas but upon the force of moral right." Continuing his line of spiritual reasoning, the president concluded with a stirring appeal to the civil faith:

Above the pyramid on the great seal of the United States it says—in Latin—"God has favored our undertaking."

God will not favor everything that we do. It is rather our duty to divine His will. But I cannot help believing that He truly understands and that He really favors the undertaking that we begin here tonight.[37]

Three months later Congress passed the Voting Rights Act of 1965 by an overwhelming majority.

Civil Religion—A Positive Force   It seems clear from the foregoing that the civil faith often has played a beneficial role in American public life, especially in the twentieth century. It provides an element of cement in an increasingly heterogeneous, pluralistic society that is in danger of centrifugal disintegration. It stands in judgment over the state and its officials and calls them back to first principles. It is a force for social justice—or at least should be. Through the notion of covenant, it supplies a framework of meaning and direction to the nation and challenges it to fulfill its noble ideals. Civil religion symbols and concepts serve as instruments in the hands of wise political leaders to inspire the country to greater and higher levels of achievement. In many instances civil religion has functioned as a common faith for the common good.

Lutheran theologians Robert Benne and Philip Hefner insist that civil religion and its myths are necesary for the nation. In order for it to perform its function more adequately, they urge Americans to "work for its critical reformation and vivification." This will involve a theological dialog between Christians and civil religionists on such motifs as the power of the future and the sacrificial dedication which that future requires. These themes are central to both faiths, and Christians in particular can bring their understanding of evil and judgment to bear in the discussion. At the same time they can demonstrate how their concept of sacrifice as a response to evil differs markedly from the "athleticism and martyrdom" that characterizes the American dream and how they view sacrifice as a religious call to a higher way of life. They can show how it is the way mankind can grasp the future and transmute wrath into redemption. The Christian understanding of the future looks to the restoration of wholeness in the entire human community, and acts of dedication that seek to bring about this "shalom" are thereby genuinely "sacrificial actions."[38]

It is in this vein that Trueblood contends that civil religion can be considered "a valid Christianity *beyond* the Church," and it provides "extra-ecclesiastical experiences that have meaning" for those millions who have no real connection with the Christian faith. At the same time, multiple religious memberships can exist without incompatibility and, hence, "there is nothing unreasonable about the belief that God can guide a nation as truly as He guides a Church." In America "we have a vast amount of religion that is not Church religion" and regardless of how deeply we believe in the church "we can be grateful that it is not all that we have." Furthermore, one should not object to the American conviction that the entire national destiny has a "fundamentally religious character," but instead "rejoice when reverence and patriotism can be combined" because this helps to maintain "decent standards of behavior in the human family."[39]

Trueblood views civil religion in the most favorable light possible, but problems arise when he attempts to relate it to Christianity. He recognizes that American civil faith has not severed the connection with its biblical roots; nonetheless, most spokesmen for it do not mention Jesus Christ. In his opinion, there is no good reason why they should since there is and ought to be, a "clear division of function between the civil religion and Christianity." In other words, civil faith is an expression of deism that exists side by side with Christianity. Trueblood believes church religion and civil religion can help each other construct a "self-revising society" that is not ultimate in any way but always subject to higher considerations.[40]

Many feel that it is not all that simple. Is there enough room in any society for two faiths with transcendent values and a claim to higher loyalties? Can they peacefully coexist indefinitely? Or will one eventually strive to gain dominance over the other? If so, would Christianity come out on the short end in that struggle, especially in a religiously plural nation? In short, what happens when the claims of civil religion conflict with those of the Christian faith?

5

CIVIL RELIGION
AS A COMPROMISED FAITH
FOR PURPOSES OF STATE

My brothers and sisters: As we gather at this prayer breakfast let us beware of the real danger of misplaced allegiance, if not outright idolatry, to the extent we fail to distinguish between the god of an American civil religion and the God who reveals Himself in the Holy Scriptures and in Jesus Christ.

If we as leaders appeal to the god of civil religion, our faith is in a small and exclusive deity, a loyal spiritual Advisor to power and prestige, a Defender of only the American nation, the object of a national folk religion devoid of moral content. But if we pray to the Biblical God of justice and righteousness, we fall under God's judgment for calling upon His name, but failing to obey His commands.[1]

These prophetic words pronounced by Senator Mark Hatfield at the National Prayer Breakfast in 1973 epitomize the fears which many Christians have about civil religion. Is a national community held together by a deistic civil faith a threat to the spiritual health of the institutional church and individual believers? Does a virile public faith transform the nation into an idol, demanding that Christians make a choice as to where their ultimate loyalty will be placed? Is it a tool in the hands of the country's leaders which they use to manipulate the masses? Are national moral standards simply determined by political elites and communicated to the populace through the structures of civil religion? Does it serve to mask the true objective of the state, which is the accumulation of power? In short, is civil faith a substitute religion that undermines authentic belief in the transcendent Creator God who loves his creatures so much that he sent his only begotten Son to earth to redeem them through the sacrifice at Calvary? The critics of civil religion are likely to reply affirmatively to most if not all of these questions. This chapter will survey their lines of argumentation.

Civil Religion As an Ersatz Faith   First, they insist that although civil religion may resemble Christianity at many points, it is far different from the biblical faith and should be exposed as an ersatz faith, a substitute religion which has no legitimate claim to the allegiance of Jesus' disciples. They concur with Billy Graham's assessment in a Bicentennial sermon that civil religion is "nothing more than a combination of contradictory viewpoints fused into a soulless pattern of pragmatic opportunism."[2] Walfred Peterson, a respected political scientist and evangelical Christian, describes the deity of this religion as "a least-common-denominator god," one who is acceptable to people at large and who maximizes social and political unity.[3] Since the god of civil piety must not give offense to nonchurch people, the name of Christ seldom if ever appears in civic rituals and symbols. In other words, the public faith is a deistic religion, devoid of the sense of distinctiveness that normally characterizes revealed religion. Moreover, its demands can be summed up under the rubric of civil virtue—do your duty, honor your country, obey the laws, pay your debts, promote good will, practice patriotism and such things. The morality is essentially that of a works religion, one that stands diametrically opposite to the type of claim which Christ makes on the life of the individual believer.[4] The public faith requires nothing more than to be a good citizen.

Since Christ is not mentioned in acts of civic piety, distinctively Christian concepts are absent from its public pronouncements. Little or nothing is heard about such matters as sin, guilt, confession, repentance and the final end of the human race. Dr. Eugene S. Callender, the 1973 National Church Preacher of the United Presbyterian denomination, suggests that civic piety is a "religion of order, of law, of national unity, of uncriticized values and priorities; justice and right are more prominent than salvation and love." To put it another way, a religion has grown up alongside Christianity that superficially resembles it, overlaps it at some points, but deviates from it in essential respects. Unfortunately, many American Christians fail to recognize this difference, and they allow both the flag and the cross to arouse in them the same sentiments.[5] "Civil religion's unitarianism ignores the scandal of the cross, the exclusiveness of biblical religion, and the particularity of the religion which insists that God has shown humanity his face in Jesus Christ," so argues Southern Baptist leader Foy Valentine.[6]

Some Christians are uneasy about the tendency of American civil theology to lose sight of the just and transcendent God who is above all nations and to make the nation itself the object of ultimate loyalty. It frequently becomes the center of the individual citizen's aspirations, dreams and values, and serves as the standard for all other institutions in society, such as the church, home and business. The designs of the Almighty are regarded as identical with the goals of the nation, and in the United States this means that the God of the Bible often is packaged as a red, white and blue middle-class American product. Civil religion is thus an amalgamation of generalized faith, Christianity and Americanism which equates God's will with the American system. Political science professor Perry Cotham insists that church members frequently fail to distinguish between the Christian and the national way, and that they

> work in concert with other American institutions to give
> sanctity to middle-class values and political principles;
> they purport to be Christian, but they would choose Amer-

icanism and the interests of the middle class if they could
be convinced that genuine Christianity and their watered-
down version of it are different.[7]

Martin Marty ventures the opinion that the god of Christian
Americanism is a "harmless little divinity" who has nothing
in common with the God of the Bible. He is "understandable
and manageable," cozy and comforting and one of us, an
"American jolly good fellow."[8] Mennonite sociologist Donald Kraybill adds that this tribal deity is very slow to anger,
an all-round "nice guy" who is especially fond of American
sports—like football and baseball—and he thrives on public
displays of piety.[9]

In other words, these commentators fear that as an all-
powerful God is de-emphasized, the religious transcendence
of the civil faith will drift inexorably in the direction of
idolatry. When the nation is enthroned alongside God, true
religion is undermined and eventually the transcendent
state becomes a substitute for the transcendent God of the
universe. Finally, America will be deified and the state will
transgress on territory that is God's. Callender delineates
the impact of civil religion in eloquent but shocking terms:

> Civil religion blunts the faith of the Christian Church by
> substituting a vague providence for an explicit historical
> revelation; it tends to reduce so-called revealed religion
> to a private matter, thus pushing church life to the periph-
> ery of public life; it so stresses the pluralism of American
> churches as to suggest that civic religion alone can pro-
> vide national community; it substitutes its own rituals for
> those of the churches and synagogues gradually replacing
> them by a ceremonial piety that has qualitatively different
> values; it draws on biblical analogies but it distorts their
> prophetic power and imagery in the national interest.[10]

The Handmaiden of the State   Senator Hatfield has called
the practice of using religion to legitimize political leaders
the "sin of Uzziah." He was the king of Judah described in
2 Chronicles 26 who, contrary to God's law and on his own

initiative, burned incense in the temple and immediately was struck down with leprosy as punishment. Hatfield contends that civil religion in this regard helps make "the authority and power of the state absolute and supreme, even above our loyalty to God's laws and instructions." It claims divine blessing on the state and assumes that "loyalty to God always means total loyalty to the state." In essence it is a modern-day type of civil theocracy in which God is put "on the throne of our land instead of on the throne of our lives."[11]

The critics call attention to a number of ways in which the state and its officials exploit civil religion for their own purposes. For one thing, it can serve to comfort the political order by assuring those in charge that God "is on their side." Peterson explains that this is done by defining God in terms of national life. He is portrayed as a deity who unites the citizens and urges them to practice the civil virtues needed for a smoothly operating state.[12] In the American context the custom is to tell people that they belong to a nation which has a special relationship with God and which thereby possesses a distinctive spirituality. Since the deity controls the national destiny, Americans can take confidence in the realization that they play a crucial role in the working out of the divine will in the world.

The common faith also may be employed to undergird the status quo. By identifying God's purposes with a nation's way of life, the present existence can be viewed as being in accordance with the divinely established plan and all attempts to change political and social structures rejected as ultimately striking at God himself. This impels the radical Christian journalist Jim Wallis to declare that civil religion has "little capacity to bring a word of judgment or correction to a social order." It merely provides a religious justification for the society and serves "as the ideological glue" which holds the social system together in consensus and conformity.[13]

During the Eisenhower years William Lee Miller called attention to the way that politicians were taking a great deal of

interest in "official religion." This phenomenon, which in
the following decade would more commonly be called "civil
religion," was a mixture of patriotism and religious behavior
that was intended to serve "the purposes of a conservative
social philosophy, as when the old ways in faith bless the old
ways in economics.... The direction in which God is to be
found is 'back.' "[14] This means the solution for all modern
problems is to "get back to God"—that is, affirm things as
they are, or used to be. Needless to say, these commentators
would point out that such a status quo religion contrasts
dramatically with the actions of both the Old Testament
prophets and the New Testament evangelists.

They are especially distressed by those situations in
which Christians find themselves being misused by the
leaders of the state. This may result when they either uncriti-
cally regard the policies of the national leaders as being in
harmony with God's intentions or are simply overawed by
pious actions on the part of the political elite. One example
is the 1970 Honor America Day "religious service"—precisely the expression used in the *Christianity Today* news
report—mentioned previously in chapter three. Many observers at the time interpreted it as a show of support for the
Nixon Administration and its policies, and some openly
criticized Billy Graham for lending his voice to this act of
civil religion. They pointed out that in his address at the
Lincoln Memorial, America's leading evangelist exhorted
his audience to honor their country, raise their voices in
prayer and dedication to God and recommit themselves to
the ideals and dreams on which the country was founded.
He implored them to shun extremism and urged that they
"never give in" to those who were critical of old-fashioned
American virtues and, by implication, of the president's
Vietnam policy.

Even so-called nonpolitical evangelical functions may fall
prey to the enticements of civil religion if vigilance is not
exercised. For instance, in June 1972 Campus Crusade for
Christ sponsored a massive evangelistic and training pro-

gram in Dallas, Texas called EXPLO '72. The organizers, apparently feeling that the eighty thousand young people assembled there needed a good dose of patriotism, made sure that Flag Day (June 14) did not pass unnoticed. High-ranking military officers, chaplains, families of men who were missing in action and prisoners of war in Vietnam and even an astronaut were given seats of honor to view the ceremony as it unfolded in the Cotton Bowl. The U.S. Navy chief of chaplains led in prayer, while a four-star general gave a brief history of Flag Day and the U.S. Army. The general drew a thunderous round of applause from the crowd when he confessed that he had dedicated his life to Christ. A color guard representing each military service carried flags into the stadium, and the delegates recited the Pledge of Allegiance. (What the participants who were not United States citizens did at this point was not reported.) A handful of demonstrators called for an end to the war but they promptly were silenced by those seated nearby. Since President Nixon earlier had sent the gathering a lengthy telegram assuring them of his "prayers" and Billy Graham had introduced a "spokesman" from South Vietnam who described the situation there as a holy war against the Viet Cong, some have concluded, perhaps incorrectly but with some justification, that this had been staged to generate enthusiasm for the Nixon administration's endeavors.[15]

Another striking illustration of how Christians may be enticed by civil religion was the joint convention of the National Association of Evangelicals and National Religious Broadcasters which took place in Washington in February 1976. Standing beneath a huge red, white and blue banner embellished with the words "Let Freedom Ring," speaker after speaker extolled the glories of America. However, the most spectacular event of all in this conclave—significantly labeled in press accounts as "a festival of civil religion"—was the appearance of President Ford. The timing was hard to miss—only a few days before the crucial primary elections in New Hampshire and Florida—and he took advantage of the opportunity to curry favor among the country's alleged forty million evangelicals.

The audience of four thousand gave the president a standing ovation as he recalled examples of faith in the lives of the nation's founders and offered what he felt was the real answer to corruption and widespread distrust in the institutions of society: "We can believe in God. We can believe in the faith of our fathers. . . . It will live as long as freedom rings in this sweet land of liberty." After Ford completed his remarks, Southern Baptist minister Jess Moody, clasping hands with the president, led in prayer, asking God to "teach us that the United States is called U.S. because it is a gift to us from you. . . . Lord, we thank you for thinking of the idea called America." In the face of all of this, "hundreds wept for joy!"[16]

Perhaps the most controversial instance in recent years where religious sentiment was utilized for political purposes was former President Nixon's White House worship services. The chief executive claimed he wanted "to emphasize the country's basic faith in a Supreme Being" and one way to do this was to set a good example by holding Sunday worship in the presidential mansion.[17] As indicated earlier, these services were hardly times of national or personal self-examination. Instead of hearing the words of a modern Amos or Isaiah, the president was treated to such pleasantries as Norman Vincent Peale's comment on Father's Day that it was "a privilege to preach in the presence of the first father of the nation." And his ears were tickled by the likes of Rabbi Louis Finklestein who prayed that "the future historian looking back on our generation may say . . . that in a period of great tribulations, the finger of God pointed to Richard Milhous Nixon, giving him the vision and the wisdom to save the world and civilization."[18] Seldom were more innocuous—some would say sycophantic—sermons delivered than at these functions.

Nixon's foes were convinced that these White House gatherings encouraged people to identify organized religion with national values and the president's policies. The speakers and audience were carefully chosen in order not to constitute any threat to the prestige of their host. And nothing was said that might have called Nixon's actions into question. All was sweetness and light in the country's "most prestigious house church," as one wag put it. Even as the United States sank ever more deeply into the morass of first Vietnam and then Watergate, the White House preachers remained silent about the transgressions of national leaders. They had been compromised and neutralized by their cozy relationships with those in places of political power and reduced to the status of handmaidens of the state.

Distortion of the National Experience   Thirty-five years ago Vice President Henry A. Wallace delivered an address entitled "Why Did God Make America?" in which he asserted:

> Who can say that the prophet did not have America in his mind and the present day in his heart when he envisions the sun as a "Sun of righteousness"? ... America, without pride of race but with complete tolerance and great power, can be that "Sun of righteousness" with healing in its wings. America can establish the time of truly great peace and justice to all the peoples.[19]

Captured in these few words is the essence of the modern messianic vision of America, a serious distortion of the national experience. Detractors of civil religion claim that the concept of national mission is an integral part of its belief system and that its expression has done inestimable harm to America's image as the standard-bearer of freedom and justice in the world.

Edward McNall Burns writes in *The American Idea of Mission* that "one of the principal clues to knowledge of America is the sense of mission which has run like a golden thread through most of her history."[20] As pointed out in chapter two, Americans more than most peoples conceived of their nation as ordained to guide and instruct others in justice and righteousness and to carry civilization to the backward, benighted regions of the globe. They were a New Israel, responsible for achieving a maximum of liberty and democracy in their own society and helping the rest of mankind to benefit from the American example. Herman Melville eloquently summed up this feeling in his midnineteenth-century novel *White-Jacket*:

> We Americans are the peculiar, chosen people—the Israel of our time; we bear the ark of the liberties of the world. . . . God has predestined, mankind expects, great things from our race; and great things we feel in our souls. The rest of the nations must soon be in our rear. We are the pioneers of the world; the advance-guard, sent on through the wilderness of untried things, to break a new path in the New World that is ours. . . . The political Messiah . . . has come in us, if we would but give utterance to his promptings. And let us always remember that with ourselves, almost for the first time in the history of earth, national selfishness is unbounded philanthropy; for we cannot do a good to America, but we give alms to the world.[21]

The concept of American mission was applied at different times to different causes, such as continental expansionism in the 1840s, the preservation of the Union during the Civil War, imperialism in 1898-1900, making the world safe for democracy in 1917, the struggle for a better international order in World War 2, anticommunism during the Cold War and the New Frontier and Great Society idealism of the Kennedy-Johnson years. But the belief was simple. God had called forth some hardy souls from the old, privilege-ridden nations, and carried them to a new world where the environment was ideally suited for them and their descendants to develop a free society. He bestowed on them the responsibility for the success of popular institutions. If their experiment failed, all people wanting or deserving of freedom would be the worse off. In short, America was commissioned to be the "testament to freedom," the "laboratory of democracy."[22]

In its finest sense the idea of mission makes America the servant of all mankind. But there is a more seamy, secularized side to it as well. A feeling of mission reinforced by religious sentiments may turn America into a messianic policeman who seeks to remake the world in its own image. Mission in this manner becomes a fusion of civic piety and belief in God which is directed against other peoples and their political and economic systems. America's actions are regarded as divinely directed and its citizens expect God to be on their side at all times. Historian John Warwick Montgomery is convinced that the Founding Fathers' belief that America was God's chosen nation "permitted subsequent generations to view other people as necessarily inferior, less receptive to divine grace, less within God's plan for the ages —and fair game if they opposed our national interests."[23]

Critics note that examples of this kind of attitude have appeared in several evangelical Bicentennial tomes. For example, Dale Evans Rogers affirms in her recent book of civil piety, *Let Freedom Ring!*:

It was never in the destiny of 400,000 red men to have and hold dominion over a land promised to greatness and power in the world. Its vastness was too much for one race. Yet the Indian did represent a long step forward in the divine purpose; he was a vast improvement upon the beast, for he sensed the presence of invisible gods and spirits all around him. . . .

But even their Great Spirit could not save them from the relentless attack of a new brand of man who came against them. . . . The white man brought weapons of iron and gunpowder, axes that leveled their forests, ploughs that cut deep into the earth—and Bibles. The scattered, wandering tribes fought desperately to stem the tide but they could not possibly win. They were forced out, in the words of Jesse Hays Baird "by cosmic forces beyond the control of any man or nation."[24]

The imperialistic drive with its patronizing approach toward "our little brown brothers" that runs in a direct line from the

Philippines to Vietnam may be singled out as another example of civil religion gone astray. Congregationalist minister and social gospel figure Josiah Strong wrote in 1886 that the Anglo-Saxon, the great representative of the two ideas that enabled mankind to reach the highest level of civilization (pure spiritual Christianity and civil liberty), was "divinely commissioned" to be his brother's keeper. This powerful race, "having developed peculiarly aggressive traits calculated to impress its institutions upon mankind," would spread over the earth and "move down upon Mexico, down upon Central and South America, out upon the islands of the sea, over upon Africa and beyond." The "extinction of inferior races before the advancing Anglo-Saxon" appeared probable, and there was no doubt that "the result of this competition of races would be 'the survival of the fittest.' "[25]

That which was only theoretical became actualized in the Spanish-American War when many voices from the Christian community urged the God of battles to avenge the sinking of the *Maine*. Numerous other Christian leaders suggested that the United States at least should play the benevolent role of the good Samaritan toward abused Spanish subjects in the Caribbean and the Far East. For instance, commenting on the spectacular victory at Manila Bay in 1898, noted pulpiteer Lyman Abbott exuberantly proclaimed:

> Not in Old Testament History is there record of a battle in which more clearly and strikingly is manifested the Divine Providence leading up to it and a Divine sanction issuing from it than in that most extraordinary battle of all time, in which one fleet [the Spanish] is utterly destroyed, and not a ship seriously injured, and not a life lost on the other side [the American].[26]

President William McKinley acted in the tradition of civil religion to vindicate America's action in the Spanish conflict. After the triumph at Santiago he issued a proclamation requesting that people offer prayers of thanksgiving on their next day of worship and suggested that they

should reverently bow before the throne of Divine Grace

and give devout praise to God, who holdeth the nations in the hollow of His hands and worketh upon them the marvels of His high will, and who has thus far vouchsafed to us the light of His face and led our brave soldiers and seamen to victory.[27]

In an interview with five Methodist clergymen on November 21, 1899, the president confided that he had not planned to take the Philippines but "they came to us as a gift from the gods," they were "dropped in our laps." Deeply perplexed, he paced the floor of the White House for several evenings until midnight and went down on his knees and prayed to "Almighty God for light and guidance more than one night." Finally the revelation came to him that "there was nothing left for us to do but to take them all, and to educate the Filipinos, and uplift and civilize and Christianize them, and by God's grace do the very best we could by them, as our fellow men for whom Christ also died. And then I went to bed, and went to sleep, and slept soundly."[28]

Needless to say, McKinley had extensive backing from Christian leaders in America. To cite one example, the president went to his customary place of worship, the Metropolitan Methodist Church in Washington, on the Sunday after Santiago and heard Dr. Frank Bristol ask rhetorically:

Were the guns of Dewey and Sampson less providential than the ram's horns of Joshua, the lamps and pitchers of Gideon, or the rod of Moses? Were Manila and Santiago less providential in the history of human freedom than Jericho and Ai? Is Christian civilization less providential than was Jewish barbarism?

If God ever had a peculiar people He has them now. They are the product of all the struggles and aspirations of the past. The men who stand before Santiago are not the product of a day or a century. They are the rich, consummate flower of the ages, the highest evolution of history. They represent a manhood that has climbed century by century up the steeps of light and liberty, and now

stands in sight of the glorified summits of the universal freedom and universal brotherhood of men.[29]
The preceding reinforces the assumption that a secularized, messianic sense of national mission undercuts the positive benefits of America as a "city upon a hill" and opens the door for a more muscular approach which seeks to impose American values, institutions and commercial enterprise on other peoples.[30] As his remarks in a 1973 college commencement address clearly show, Senator Hatfield shares this view: "The promised land becomes a perfect land" and this gives Americans "a sense of righteous mission to the world." The country's actions become "spiritually ordained," and even in war its people "are beyond reproach, fulfilling some divine destiny." Speaking specifically about the Vietnam conflict from which the United States had just withdrawn, the Oregon lawmaker stressed: "An American civil religion wants us to believe there is honor in the peace we have achieved; that this past war can be vindicated, that what we have done was necessary and right, and that we can be proud of it."[31] For many Americans, the conviction that their country has a unique role to play in the world has been transformed by modern catchall civil religion from an evangelical "city upon a hill" into a secularized cop to make the world safe for capitalism.

One Nation under God   Many evangelical scholars are concerned about the impact civil religion has had on the way in which their fellow believers in the United States perceive the flow of their nation's history. Already alluded to in the opening chapter, the basic assumption of this outlook is, as one evangelical pastor put it, that the country was founded "upon Christian principles" as a "holy experiment by people who had faith in Jesus Christ."[32]

Drawing from a wide range of works by evangelical scholars, preachers and popular writers, it is possible to outline a Special Providence of God theory of American history that is inspired by civil religion categories and widely accepted in principle, if not in every detail, by conservative Protestants in the United States. What follows is an outline of that theory.

According to Norman Vincent Peale, "America has had a unique background of faith from its very beginning." The men and women who built this country "have been moved by a spiritual zeal that continues to influence the character and purpose of our life today."[33] More eloquent is Dale Rogers's contention that America "was no historical or geographical accident; it was an idea in the mind of God before it became earthly reality.... It was—and is—a part of His purpose for mankind."[34] Well-known Christian author and businessman George Otis affirms: "God's hand was in the founding of this country, and the fiber of Christ is in the very fabric of America."[35] In Pastor Tim LaHaye's view, the people who established the United States were "Bible-oriented Christians" motivated by a spiritual dynamic.[36] Edward Elson succinctly characterizes this force:

> We cannot understand America except as a spiritual movement. The eternal God is the source of this nation ... and his Spirit the guide of its development.... When true to her genius she has a spiritual destiny—a sense of mission derived from faith in the sovereign God.[37]

The first settlers brought a distinctly Christian conception of life to the New World, and this was firmly imbedded in many institutions they created. However, their religious convictions proved to be shallow, and creative leadership was stifled within the establishment. Hence, the most important forerunners of American democracy were actually the Dissenters—a "freedom triumvirate" of "Bible-believing evangelicals"—Roger Williams, Thomas Hooker and William Penn.[38] But, as spiritual vitality gradually waned among the later colonials, a revival became imperative. God sent a time of refreshing—the Great Awakening of the 1730s and 1740s —and preachers such as Jonathan Edwards and George Whitefield brought thousands to Christ, thereby laying the moral basis for the coming revolution. As former *Decision*

editor Sherwood Wirt expressed it, a direct result of the
revival

> was a mighty infusion of confidence into the colonies.
> Early Americans learned to think for themselves. A cli-
> mate for independence was created as the people became
> convinced that the sovereignty of God gave them the
> ability and the capacity to govern themselves. After decid-
> ing for Christ they went on to decide their destiny.[39]

Because the Great Awakening "established the necessity of
men serving God as their conscience dictated—not as the
state decreed" and provided the vision of a better society,[40]
the colonists became increasingly unhappy with the tyranny
of king and parliament and finally opted for independence.
The godly, courageous Americans pledged their lives, fortunes and sacred honor in the noble cause of the revolution
in a fashion analogous to what Christ had done in his day.
Or as Alabama Baptist public official Lambert Mims put it,
"Our freedom from the curse of sin cost God His only begotten Son. Our American freedom cost our forefathers and it
cost the men who signed the Declaration [of Independ-
ence]."[41]

In the forefront of the struggle were evangelical preachers
and lay people, the best known of whom was Peter Muhlenberg, a Lutheran pastor in Virginia. After accepting a
colonel's commission, he dramatically took leave of his congregation by preaching a fiery sermon calling for armed resis-
tance. At the benediction he removed his clerical robe, revealing himself to the people in full military dress, and then
stepped down from the pulpit and signed up recruits for his
regiment. The divine hand at work in the revolution was also
evident at the time General Washington faced almost certain
destruction at Valley Forge during the cruel winter of 1777.
His supplies were nearly exhausted and his forces substantially outnumbered by the British. But instead of despairing,
he knelt in prayer and God intervened to save his gallant
soldiers. In the words of Billy Graham: "Out of that turning to
God came the solution to the problems of the Revolutionary

War, and ultimate victory."[42]

Once independence was achieved, the founders (at the instigation of Benjamin Franklin) sought divine assistance as they drafted the Constitution. The result of their labors was a document unlike any other one in history because it created a government of laws rather than of men. Further, the basic character of the new nation agreed "exactly with the purposes and principles of government ordained by Scripture," and "the principles of the teachings of Christ" were incorporated into it.[43] That is, the republic was founded on the moral law given to mankind in the Decalogue and confirmed and added to by the New Testament. It recognized the existence of God, the government's dependence on him for authority to rule over men and the depravity of man, as evidenced by the checks and balances built into the system.[44] The Founding Fathers "agreed unanimously that democracy, with all its inherent freedoms, could not thrive without a strong moral base," and so they looked to God, "the only sure foundation upon which to build a nation that would endure."[45] As the significant documents of the founding period so clearly manifest, these statesmen repeatedly expressed their deep faith in God.

Moreover, in the early days of the republic the nation's leaders relied on God for their strength and often spent time in prayer and fasting. However, a mood of skepticism started to settle over the land, but then God intervened on behalf of his people. Revival broke out both on Eastern college campuses and at frontier camp meetings, and a tremendous spiritual movement, known to historians as the Second Great Awakening, swept the country. Further times of refreshing followed in times of crisis, such as the "prayer meeting revival" in 1858 and the great evangelistic endeavors of D. L. Moody. Thus, the history of God's American Israel paralleled that of ancient Israel—"a pattern of drifting away from God followed by a period of renewal and revival," sums up Christian Reformed writer John F. De Vries.[46]

The Lord sustained his people through the greatest trial of

all, the Civil War, by sending Lincoln to preside over the nation. In the opinion of *Moody Monthly* director Robert Flood: "No other President so consistently demonstrated, and so deeply believed" as he "that the Almighty God of the universe rules in the affairs of men." Lincoln possessed a deep "awareness of his need and dependence on One higher than himself." He knew the Bible well, quoted it with ease and made it an integral part of his thought patterns. As the wartime crisis deepened he turned more and more to the Bible and prayer. It is probable that if divine Providence had placed the reins of leadership in the hands of a person of lesser stature and integrity, the Union would not have survived and the United States would have ended up on the scrap heap of history.[47]

During the nineteenth century the country flourished on the principles of biblical Christianity, such as the sovereignty of God, divinely revealed law, God-given freedom of the individual and the benevolent direction of the Almighty.[48] Unlimited opportunity made it possible for those who worked hard and sought divine help to improve their social and economic standing. Nearly all successful people in political, economic and cultural life were God-fearing, and they cherished Christian virtues like industry, honor, integrity and thrift. Presidents in particular acknowledged their dependence on God and sought divine guidance during their administrations.

So long as Americans walked in God's ways, he faithfully poured out his bounties upon them and kept them a free people.[49] But as their wealth increased, they forgot the God who made them and strayed ever further from the path of national righteousness. The American character and the former attentiveness to God's purposes fell by the wayside in the late nineteenth century. The Lord, however, did not remain indifferent to the apostasy of his people, and even as the land was experiencing unparalleled prosperity, he spoke in judgment—World War 1, the Russian Revolution, the Great Depression and World War 2. Yet, America refused to turn from its wicked ways and continued to live off the past accumulation of spiritual and moral strength. Unwilling to heed God's prophets who called for repentance, the United States slipped ever deeper into the quicksand of iniquity. In this context the Bicentennial in particular became a time when America was challenged to return to the God of its fathers.

Crime in the streets, pornography, abortion on demand, drug abuse, homosexuality, the occult, the youth rebellion and women's liberation are symptoms of the spiritual malaise. According to some exponents of this interpretation, a subtle shift has taken place from the republican conception of the founders to modern-day democracy—"the junking of America," as Rus Walton of the now defunct Third Century Publishers sees it—and the people have traded their faith in the absolute power of God for faith in the all-powerful state.[50] As a result, the government currently is strangling free enterprise, the welfare state is pushing the country toward bankruptcy and secularism and racial integration are destroying the public schools. As the country's military posture steadily deteriorates, the monster of world communism continues to crush free peoples everywhere and America's own survival is in jeopardy.

Viewing the wreckage of America during the Bicentennial year, Billy Graham sadly reminded Christians that spiritual apostasy and moral decay go together. Americans today, he contended, are irresponsible. They are neither grateful to Almighty God nor to the heroes of yesterday who bought their freedoms at the price of blood. The "dangers of despotism and national degradation" are increasing, and the "pages of history show plainly that apostasy and absence of patriotism make any people putty in the hands of the willful and the wicked."[51]

Robert Flood, pointing to the resurgence of biblical Christianity in the 1970s, insists that "the evangelical threads of American history still hold, because God has seen to it."[52] But Charles Blair, pastor of the mammoth Calvary Temple in

Denver, more pessimistically concludes: "It is bad enough for a nation to forsake God, but woe to the nation that is forsaken by God."[53] At this point it is clear that evangelicals are seriously divided over whether the United States can be saved or not. While some commentators hold out no hope for the country, many concerned Christians observed the Bicentennial by organizing prayer campaigns and sponsoring rallies to call the nation "back to God." Invariably they appealed to the spiritual heritage perceived in this popular evangelical understanding of America's past.[54]

As they plead for national repentance such people underscore the great potential for good that the United States has. For example, Otis insists that God still loves America and wants to bless it for the following reasons:

1. Twenty-four hours a day the Gospel is preached over radio and television somewhere in this country through religious programming. God honors this constant voice of truth which whispers night and day to the moral conscience of the nation.

2. We are the only country with the inscription, "In God We Trust," stamped upon our coinage. In spite of our moral plunge, this reference to God passes through our hands daily, and serves as a constant reminder to the trust which was once the very foundation of our country.

3. Many of the world's greatest missions have been founded by Americans.

4. Americans by far offer the most financial support to the work of world evangelism.

5. America has paid out over 200 billion dollars to the needy people of the world, even to its defeated enemies, such as Germany and Japan.

6. During all of America's history she has taken in the homeless aliens of other lands.[55]

Professional historians whose religious convictions lay outside the realm of evangelical Christianity are likely to regard the preceding interpretation as rather naive. Of course this view of the nation's past springs from the heartfelt desire of many devout Christians, especially those whose political orientation is conservative, to restore the close link between civic faith and biblical Christianity which existed in the era of the evangelical consensus. Unfortunately, they have not grasped fully the implications of the demise of the old Protestant order and the establishment of a much more secular and pluralistic civil religion in the twentieth century. Therefore, critics feel justified in suggesting that their understanding of America is out of touch with much of the past and with present realities.

America Is Not God's Elect Nation   Evangelicals who are embarrassed by this view of American history argue that civil religion has distorted how their fellow Christians understand the past, and they are quick to offer reasons why it is defective. First, they make the point that it is too simplistic to emphasize only the religious motives of the Colonial Americans and to maintain that they founded a "Christian nation." Further, the ideological components of the revolution were drawn as much from Enlightenment deism as evangelical Christianity. The creed of the Founding Fathers was that all men were equal in their claim to justice, that governments existed to give justice and their authority therefore was just. The Creator was the ultimate source of these equal rights, but he did not intervene in any sort of supernatural way to guarantee their preservation. Newcomers were welcomed into the nation upon profession of faith in the American democratic way of life and belief in the national creed. Much was left unsaid in the founding documents, such as any mention of the all-pervasiveness of sin, the need for redemption through Christ's atoning death and the inability of people to save themselves through civil righteousness. After analyzing the religious beliefs of the various revolutionary leaders, John Montgomery cautions his evangelical readers against clinging to the idea that most of the Founding Fathers were "believing Christians." This view, he says, is "very largely a pious myth."[56]

To declare, as Rus Walton does, that the Constitution is "divinely-inspired" and that it set up a "government resting squarely on Christian principles,"[57] not only shocks the sensibilities of many believers, but also casts doubt on the infallibility and immutability of divine truth itself. After all, the Constitution was written by mortals and it bears the marks of the framers' humanity. Although the authors of the Constitution correctly gauged the forces that would try to exercise power and they developed a system to neutralize these—an action commensurate with the biblical doctrine of human sinfulness—the Constitution being a manmade political document displays the scars of compromise and thus cannot qualify as an "ideal expression of Christian ideas." The statements in Article I, Section 2 that a slave counts as only "three-fifths" of a man for purposes of apportionment and in Article IV, Section 2 that fugitive slaves must be surrendered to their owners are examples of such compromises. Slavery was legally acknowledged, slaves officially were considered subhuman and many people who bore the image of God were regarded merely as property.[58]

Other defects were present in the original document, not all of which can be brushed aside as technicalities. For instance, it tacitly allowed the poll tax which discriminated against the poor and racial minorities and denied suffrage to women. The Constitution has been amended several times to rectify these and other difficulties. It appears ironic that in a day when many evangelicals are engaged in a "battle for the Bible," others want to elevate the founding documents of the American republic to the status of Holy Writ.

A second shortcoming often mentioned by critics is that this view reverses the role of American history and Christian faith. Instead of beginning with the Scriptures, determining the directives for political life therein and applying these to the American tradition, this approach starts with American history, points out its religious aspects and concludes that America did indeed originate as a Christian nation.[59] Rather than measure the religious nature of early America against the standards set by God's Word, it simply assumes that the utilization of religious symbols and expressions by the founders of America constitutes prima-facie evidence of a national trust in God. Because the early leaders were nominally Protestants, they were as the dominant group able to inject their values into the political and social fabric of the country, ones which were not necessarily equivalent to or even the product of a transforming faith in Christ.

Third, critics emphasize that significant groups—black slaves, American Indians, Roman Catholics, Jews and immigrants from southern and eastern Europe—were largely excluded from the pale of Christian nationality in the first 150 years of the nation's history. As a result, Americans of Protestant and largely Anglo-Saxon ancestry compartmentalized their national faith in a manner that only through the most shortsighted and torturous mental gymnastics could be harmonized with a genuine biblical faith in the crucified and resurrected Christ. Slavery was justified by lifting prooftexts from the Bible, and the killing of Indians rationalized from Old Testament passages about Israel's obligation to conquer the land of Canaan. At the same time that revival swept the country in the 1830s and 1850s, anti-Catholic riots raged in northern cities and many Protestants plunged into nativist and Know-Nothing activities.

Finally, it is noted that this interpretation does not recognize that when the Founding Fathers talked about separation of church and state, they really meant pluralism and the multiplicity of religious groups. As the nation's history unfolded in the nineteenth century, it appeared that evangelical Protestant Christianity was the sole national religion and so the public schools inculcated its values in the young. But as growing numbers of immigrants of Roman Catholic and Jewish persuasion found new homes in America, their religious convictions challenged the Protestant consensus, and eventually the full protection of the constitutional guarantee of religious freedom was extended to cover them as well. Over the years the national religion of

America became increasingly more latitudinarian both in its civic symbolism and its expression in the public schools. Teaching national loyalty became more important in the schools than instilling religious faith and morality. Christians continued to give allegiance to what actually was a despiritualized civil religion, but they seldom realized how far the national faith had deviated from a biblical one.

Civil Religion—A Negative Force The opponents of civil religion are largely in agreement with Bellah's contention that the American variety "has often been used and is being used today as a cloak for petty interests and ugly passions."[60] They look upon the institutional church as possibly the principal victim of this development, feeling that it is being utilized to propagate unwittingly the substitute gospel of Americanism. National symbols, especially the flag, adorn the church sanctuaries of the land almost like icons, and patriotic hymns and sermons are a regular feature of the church's commemoration of national holidays. This seemed particularly to be the case during the Bicentennial observance when a vast quantity of literary material lauding the achievements of America and expounding on the nation's Christian heritage rolled off the evangelical presses. These themes were picked up in sermons, prayer campaigns and patriotic religious rallies, as America was summoned to repent and return to God.

Critics were distressed at the way in which a host of individualistic sins were denounced—drugs, alcohol, pornography, abortion, homosexuality, violent crime, gambling and so forth—and how conservatives used the occasion to attack measures insuring the rights of racial minorities and women, government-sponsored welfare programs, labor unions and world peace initiatives. But at the same time, white-collar crime by businessmen went unnoticed, the ongoing destruction of the environment was ignored, military spending continued to skyrocket, the economic and social problems of the lower socioeconomic groups were brushed aside and most regrettable of all, people looked the other way as the specter of famine and mass starvation stalked the world. Here were the national sins about which Christians should be concerned, but their attention was distracted by the compromised faith known as civil religion.

During the Bicentennial, Hatfield warned his national compatriots about the danger "of confusing God's blessing on our country with the idea that he has uniquely blessed it," and insisted that the conception of America as the New Israel too easily blends into the "our country, right or wrong" heresy.[61] He rejected the stance that civil religion is simply a generalized and often helpful belief which stimulates reflection on spiritual values and provides useful ethical guides for the country. Since it lacks the centrality of God's revelation in Jesus Christ as well as the prophetic dimension of biblical faith, Hatfield deems it "highly vulnerable to being exploited as a tool of national self-righteousness and even idolatry."[62] Such a faith serves the purposes of state without really calling it to account for its penchant to abuse power and its failure to provide justice.

Rather than submit to the God of the Scriptures and bring their political, social and economic philosophies in line with his demands for justice, proponents of civil religion have conjured up the caricature of a god. It is a shadowy divinity which Garth Rosell describes as "constructed by compromise and consensus to fit unobtrusively into every man's religious philosophy. It is a human god, conformed to the image of our culture—a convenience deity to be hauled out at political rallies and national celebrations. It is a god whose arm is shortened, who cannot save."[63]

The god of civil religion is not the God of the Bible who stands in judgment over every aspect of American culture and whose only Son gave his life to redeem men and women from all nations of the earth to be "a chosen race, a royal priesthood, a holy nation, God's own people," that they might declare the wonderful deeds of him who called them out of darkness into his marvelous light (1 Pet. 2:9).

6
TWILIGHT OF THE SAINTS OR DAWN OF A NEW DAY?

What have God's saints to do with American civil religion? Should the people of God participate to any degree in the national faith? If so, to what extent? If not, why not? Are there guidelines for believers living in a sick society? Can love for God be reconciled with love for country? What is at stake in today's world if evangelical Christians do not face up to these and related questions? Is it—as in midseventeenth-century England—the end of an era, the twilight of the saints, or is America on the brink of a time of national rejuvenation, thanks to the prayerful efforts of faithful followers of Jesus Christ?

God's saints, of course, are those whom the New Testament designates as "new people" in Christ.[1] The very word *saint* itself means one who has been called and set apart by God's Spirit as a "new creation" to live the Christian life in the world. The English Puritans had a strong identification with their role as God's new people, the saints. They conceived of politics for the moment as the pursuit of a religious goal: its end was joy! Flushed with success early in the Civil War years, Puritan poet John Milton wrote in 1644: "God is decreeing to begin some new and great period in his Church, ev'n to the reforming of Reformation itself."[2] It is only against this backdrop of great expectations that the disappointed

sentiments of John Owen a few years later can be understood:
"The summer is ended, and the harvest is past, and we are
not refreshed."[3] To Owen the twilight of the saints was
synonymous with the twilight of the Puritan religious and
political experiment. Is the same also to be true of late twentieth-century America?

The English Puritan attempts to establish a republican
commonwealth and the American Puritan effort to create a
new society in the wilderness are not only related historically, but they offer remarkable parallels in historical development. The major difference is that the English experiment
lasted only a little more than a decade while the American
attempt to build a "city upon a hill" has persisted for two
hundred years. Perhaps it is because of these similarities in
national experience that G. K. Chesterton as an English
visitor could sniff the republican air of America and with
some historical assurance declare it to be "a nation with the
soul of a church." Also, an examination of the parallels between the history of the English commonwealth and the
growth of the American republic may yield some instructive
lessons for today, at least in terms of mistakes that can be
avoided.

In this context the most haunting question is whether we
in America today are living in the period of the twilight of
the saints. Is it a time similar to that observed and lamented
by Owen in 1652 in England? Do we stand at the end of a long
era of evangelical Christian influence in American politics
and society? Or on the brighter side, are we at the dawning of
a new day of evangelical participation in the life of the nation? Will the current resurgence of biblical faith, which a
number of students of the religious scene in America have
noted, result in a new day with further opportunities for the
saints?[4] It is to these and related questions that we now turn.

Perhaps the place to begin is to reiterate the fact that since
World War 2 America has been engulfed in widescale and
serious social unrest, a matter which was discussed at length
in chapter one. At this point we want to suggest that evan-

gelicals living in a crumbling society are faced with certain alternatives. Moreover, we believe that the option which the majority of Christians in this country embrace in the next decade will be a major—perhaps *the* decisive—factor in determining the political future of the nation of America itself.

The Problem of America As a "Christian Nation" Before we outline these alternatives, we feel it is necessary to urge believers to divest themselves of the myth that America is a "Christian nation." If this can be done, it will clear the way for a more fully biblical view of the manner in which God deals with nations, including how he deals with the United States of America.

Some leading evangelicals, especially during the recent Bicentennial celebration, mistakenly—but no doubt with good intentions—proclaimed that America had been or still is a Christian nation. Others simply assumed this or strongly implied it in their publications and speeches.[5] The truth is that the United States never was nor is it now a Christian nation. No nation is, has been or can be a Christian nation. Political entities by their very nature fall outside the definition of Christian for they are created to govern a mixed population of believers and nonbelievers. Only the body of believers, the true church of Jesus Christ, is a "Christian nation" in the New Testament sense (1 Pet. 2:9, cf. Rom. 9).

To be sure, religion in general and Christianity in particular have had a major influence in the shaping of American history, and the evangelical involvement has been significant and often decisive. Religious values and convictions have been woven into the fabric of American life. Even the Supreme Court has acknowledged that "we make room for as wide a variety of beliefs and creeds as the spiritual needs of man deem necessary. We sponsor an attitude on the part of government that shows no partiality to any one group and that lets each flourish according to the zeal of its adherents and the appeal of its dogma."[6] At best such a view supports civil religion but it in no way proclaims that America is a Christian nation.

As noted in chapter five, the founders of New England and Pennsylvania incorporated principles derived from Christianity in their political structures. However, New England and Pennsylvania were not all of Colonial America, and there were other areas much less distinctively Christian in their founding and initial emphasis. Moreover, from a Christian perspective the history of the United States has been mixed and checkered from the very beginning. The development of America has been a story of shameful deeds committed in the name of the nation, as well as many great and humane accomplishments, of tragedies of sin and corruption as well as triumphs of grace and New Testament principles.

In short, it is proper to think of America, not as a Christian nation, but as a country with a distinctive history because of heavy evangelical influence and commitment. In other words, American Christianity constantly has been faced with the problem of sorting out faith influenced by culture and culture influenced by faith. In light of this condition, Chesterton's observation that America was "a nation with the soul of a church" becomes comprehensible. But equally understandable in view of our more realistic appraisal of the American past is the recent remark of the distinguished British-born journalist Alistair Cooke. When asked to comment on Chesterton's insightful affirmation, Cooke replied: "That's true, but it also has the soul of a whorehouse."[7]

Evangelicals need to take a long, hard, honest look at United States history and put aside any semblance of Christian jingoism. The primary need at this crucial hour is not to moan nostalgically for a return of the good old days—which may or may not have existed—but rather, for every effort to be expended to create an America which once again may command the respect and affection of people all over the world.

Alternatives for Evangelicals in a Crisis-Ridden Society
Undergirded by this more balanced and realistic interpretation of American history, evangelicals can choose more
intelligently among the alternatives facing them in the
present crisis. Obviously, the first option is to do nothing.
This has been advocated by a number of Christians who believe that politics is by definition dirty and who have withdrawn from the world to carry on "more spiritual pursuits."[8]

Other evangelical leaders have called for believers in this
country to join forces in a massive effort to "recapture
America for God." This view has been most fully articulated
by Dr. Bill Bright, head of Campus Crusade for Christ. Bright
told a Conference of Church Leaders for Prayer for the Nation
in Chicago in September 1975:

We are faced with the possibility of recapturing our
promised land. We have largely lost it. It was dedicated to
Jesus Christ. As far as I know, there has never been another
nation in history that has been dedicated to our Lord as
was this nation. . . . We have a rich heritage. But we are
losing our nation largely.[9]

He then urged his audience of evangelical luminaries to
unite in both prayer and political action in order to recover
the national educational system and the government for
Christ. He concluded by warning his hearers that if Christians did not pull together to turn the tide in the 1976 election, then the world might well "enter another 1,000 years of
darkness."[10]

Bright has somewhat modified this view since 1975 in
light of a flap within the evangelical community over his
alleged support of right-wing politicians as a means of "recapturing America for Christ." However, he still believes
that during the past twenty-five years the United States has
been in a process of disintegration, and that "our nation is in
grave trouble." It still remains to be seen whether his feeling
that 1976 would be a critical year is correct.[11]

The main difficulty with this alternative is that it raises
many of the same problems encountered by the seventeenth-

century English Puritans in their attempt to impose evangelical faith on their nation. How can American Christians possibly accomplish this and still be faithful to New Testament teachings and the Constitution? Even if believers agreed to attempt to "capture the nation for Christ," how can this be translated into political reality when twentieth-century evangelicals have had so much trouble relating Christian values to politics? Would it mean imposing right-wing politics on the nation? God forbid!

A third alternative advocated by many evangelicals is to embrace and encourage civil religion. This view is supported both by many Christian leaders and numerous other Americans who see it as the only way to salvage the country and national identity during a time of extreme social and political stress. It is hard to steer clear of the mainstream evangelical propensity to accept the notion that America is God's chosen nation with all of the implications involved. This includes the premise that 2 Chronicles 7:14 applies to the people of America rather than to the people of God in America: "If my people who are called by my name humble themselves, and pray and seek my face, and turn from their wicked ways, then I will hear from heaven, and will forgive their sin and heal their land." Or as 1976 Republican presidential aspirant Ronald Reagan put it:

> There is one thing about campaigning. We talk about how hard it is; but when you go out across the country and meet the people, you can't help but pray and remind God of that passage in II Chronicles because the people of this country are not beyond redemption. They are good people, and I believe this nation has a destiny as yet unfulfilled.[12]

The previous discussion of the myth of America as a Christian nation has called attention to the difficulties in adopting this viewpoint. Moreover, it was amply demonstrated that civil religion and Christianity are not the same thing and that civil religion actually is often at odds with some of the basic tenets of the evangelical faith.

A fourth option is simply to accept the fact that the majority of the American people are increasingly non-Christian, materialistic and pagan in their basic outlook, and thus prepare to live in a society which does not reflect Christian values or influence. This will be a new experience for evangelicals in America, but it is one already shared by the majority of believers in the remainder of the world and throughout the greater part of Christian history.[13] Nevertheless, this alternative leaves unanswered the nagging question of whether or not a society which is not undergirded by biblical values can sustain democracy. We doubt it.

We reject all of the foregoing as basically inadequate and opt for a fifth possibility; namely, that evangelicals concentrate on practicing the teachings of New Testament Christianity in the modern American setting. This approach involves avoiding participation in civil religion and embracing a lifestyle based upon the principles and precepts of the Bible. It means re-emphasizing the "city upon a hill" model but applying it only to the people of God rather than to the entire American nation. It entails recognizing that the situation in the late twentieth century is much more complex than it was in 1630 and that the geographical wilderness is now a moral and political one.

This option of unleashing biblical Christians with transcendent biblical values on society will mean presenting the whole counsel of God without apology and without restraint to Americans in all walks of life, at all levels of society and in every social and political context. It will include not only sharing the good news of redemptive grace with our fellow Americans but also attacking the realities of poverty, crime, pollution, inflation and boredom head-on with genuine Christian compassion and understanding rather than with a fog of patriotic rhetoric. It will involve not only participating in government but also divesting ourselves of traditional ideological labels in order to be free to apply Christian principles to the needs of society and to speak in God's name in judgment in response to our national sins. It will necessitate reaffirming our commitment to bring the Word of God, the mind of Christ and the power of the Spirit to bear in developing moral courage, social sensitivity and ethical responsibility as an inseparable part of citizenship as practiced by Christians.[14]

The Case against Civil Religion: The Bottom Line Plainly, then, we reject evangelical Christian participation in civil religion, no matter how innocent such an activity appears to be on the surface and regardless of how many distinguished and well-meaning Christians advocate doing so. It may be, as some argue, that civil religion at its best helps to maintain decent standards of behavior in the human family as well as to provide the social glue to keep America together in a time of deep tension. Nevertheless, Christians feel that biblical values are far superior to any kind of generalized behavioral patterns embraced by a religiously mixed populace, as the emergence of abortion as a political issue so amply demonstrates. Moreover, the responsibility of Christians in supplying the social cement for America or any other nation is peripheral. If a people accepts biblical norms and they constitute the social glue of that political organism, well and good. However, genuine Christianity cannot be compromised or twisted to fit the demands of a pluralistic society and a secular government and still remain true to Jesus Christ, no matter how well-meaning the intentions or how desirable the end.[15]

Frankly, it is not the best in civil religion which worries us, but the worst! The negative quality of civil religion is illustrated by Senator Goldwater's earlier cited response to Senator Hatfield's 1974 call for a national day of repentance, humiliation and prayer. Goldwater retorted: "Personally, I am so darn proud to be an American that I have no room to feel humiliated."[16] Contrast this with the biblical warning: "Pride goes before destruction, and a haughty spirit before a fall" (Prov. 16:18).

We would like to point out five reasons why evangelical Christians should beware of supporting civil religion. All of these have been touched upon and illustrated to some extent in the preceding chapter, but now we shall provide a systematic analysis of the case against civil religion in order to bring the entire issue into contemporary focus.

First, evangelical cohabitation with civil religion often gives the false impression that the nation, not Christ saves. It can lead to a confusion of Americanism and Christianity, both in the practice of its adherents and in the eyes of the non-Christian world. Too often, even the civil religion sloganeering which declares "in God we trust" is betrayed by an unquestioning, almost fanatical, support of larger and larger defense budgets which proclaims to the watching world that it is really "in missiles we trust." On numerous occasions evangelicals have in the name of "God and country" been bamboozled into conforming to the world and its values, and they have let those values go unchallenged. We have been hesitant to confront the problems of materialism, militarism or racism, because it would be detrimental to national interests, and in that reticence we run the danger of equating the American way with the Christian way of life. This violates the biblical injunction that we "not be conformed to this world" (Rom. 12:2).

Christian Americanism also is risky because it blurs the line of separation between church and state which our leaders in the past worked so hard to draw and maintain. Moreover, the involvement of churches in the promotion of civil religion deflects them from performing their primary tasks of evangelizing, teaching and ministry, as the continuing struggle over religion in the public schools and the quest for a prayer amendment to the Constitution so painfully testify. This preoccupation with civil religion leads many churches to display both the Christian and the American flags in their chancels, much to the consternation and amazement of visiting brothers and sisters in Christ from other lands. The presence of the country's flag in the church does much to foster the notion that Christianity is the religion of Americanism and to blur the distinction between the two.

Second, civil religion easily can become a tool which national leaders use in times of stress and unrest to drum up support for otherwise questionable policies. Exploiting or watering down religious faith in order to make it compatible with political ends is not a peculiarly American temptation, nor is it unique to this period of time. Much of the history of Christianity has witnessed the political prostitution of the faith to serve the interests of emperors, kings and various governments.

Several examples of co-optation were presented in chapter two, the most notable being the attempt of Roman Emperor Constantine I to exploit Christianity for his own ends. After his alleged conversion to Christ in the early fourth century, Constantine embarked upon a socioeconomic program which reflected his favorable attitude toward Christianity. In return for exempting the Christian clergy from taxes and military service, the church was allowed to set up a separate court system of its own and the church authorities received the right to hold property. From that time on institutional Christianity was utilized—sometimes successfully, often unsuccessfully—to buttress the Roman Empire. Whole legions of the Imperial Army were baptized en masse and sent into battle for the sake of the empire. The state began using the church shamelessly to bolster its flagging prestige all over the Mediterranean world and to justify the state's very existence and power. The Constantinian compromise created a legacy which would haunt the Christian churches from that day to the present, and even now it is difficult for many Christian groups to resist the temptation of baptizing the interests of the secular state.

In America this was exemplified by the presidents who attempted to use the churches and church leaders to back them in their prosecution of the war in Vietnam. As was mentioned in chapter three President Nixon and his aides employed the Honor America Day rally in Washington on July 4, 1970 to mobilize support for the administration's war policy. On that day honoring America and God was implicitly synonymous with sustaining Nixon's aims in Southeast Asia.

Third, evangelical participation in American civil religion makes it exceedingly difficult, if not impossible, to challenge the values of our culture. Christianity which is cheek by jowl with the establishment often finds it difficult to speak a prophetic word of judgment to that establishment. The cozy confines of the country club golf course where preacher and politician tour the links together somehow dulls the cutting edge of Paul's command: "Don't let the world around you squeeze you into its own mould, but let God re-make you so that your whole attitude of mind is changed. Thus you will prove in practice that the will of God is good, acceptable to him and perfect." (Rom. 12:2, Phillips).

This lies at the heart of the situation described by Senator Hatfield regarding his good friend Billy Graham during the Nixon administration. In the Christian lawmaker's own words:

I was deeply concerned, frankly, that Billy was running the risk of being "used" by the White House. I did not deny his call to be in a pastoral relationship with Presidents. But being a true pastor to one in power, in my view, also had to involve an awareness of how any political authorities tend to seek blessing from the Church for their policies. Thus, the Christian must maintain the duality of a pastoral and prophetic witness toward the powerful; indeed, I believe this duality is necessary in all the mission of the Church.[17]

Fourth, civil religion reduces the God of the universe to the status of a tribal god. True, the modern state is larger and much more complex than the tribe of ancient times, but the feelings and urges related to its governance are much the same. Nearly all political leaders want the assurance that God is on their side, and the best way to insure this is to create, even though done unconsciously or with good intentions, a god that is defined and circumscribed in terms of national life. The deity of civil religion unites the citizenry and implants those civic virtues necessary to maintain a strong state. However, such a tribal deity stands in stark contrast to the God of the Bible who calls his people to a separated life of witness to the powers that be.

When evangelicals become involved in civil religion, they render allegiance to this tribal god, which in turn leads to the sanctioning of national sins and misdeeds as well as positive national achievements and acts of decency. In this way American civil religion easily becomes the cornerstone of support for the status quo, thus distorting the biblical conception of the relationship between the state and our faith. It tends to enshrine our national righteousness and goals while failing to speak for the need for repentance, salvation and God's standards of justice. Ever so subtly, the Promised Land becomes the Perfect Land, and America's actions become spiritually ordained. Even in war the nation is above reproach, fulfilling its divine destiny.

Fifth and finally, civil religion easily can and often has become a vehicle of national self-righteousness and even idolatry. This is possible especially in a situation such as exists today where many of the institutional church's leaders have allowed their thinking and values to be shaped by the world. A sizable segment of our American evangelical Christianity has been captured by our culture as well. For those American believers who have embraced civil religion the danger is ever present that they will slip into idolatry and make the same mistake that German Christians did in the 1930s when they allowed their religion to become Germany; so the danger in the United States is that the religion of America will become America itself.

Examples of civil religion having gone idolatrous abound in recent American history. Several of these have been cited in this volume, such as clerical backing for World War 1, the Honor America Day extravaganza, the dramatic politico-religious events of EXPLO '72, and President Nixon's religious services in the White House. All of these illustrate a civil religion devoid of the prophetic dimension of biblical faith and the centrality of God's revelation in Jesus Christ.

It is also civil religion twisted in such a manner as to invite exploitation by the state as a tool of national self-righteousness and even idolatry.

So we come to the bottom line: the propensity of civil religion to lead Christians into idolatry. Should the churches of Jesus Christ inculcate nationalism and patriotism in the minds and hearts of their people? Is there a place for civil religion in the churches? Our answer is an emphatic *No!* Civil religion is a fetching but dangerous heresy which must be treated as such. As for true patriotism, that will flow from the righteous acts of the American nation as it makes "liberty and justice for all" a reality for its citizens.

A vital conclusion to be drawn from the American experience with civil religion is that neither pious pronouncements nor religious ceremonies produce genuine patriotism and true religion. Patriotism and Christianity do not rest upon a foundation of God-words and state ritual. Now we are obligated first to suggest positive principles for evangelicals in dealing with the claims of civil religion and second to propose steps for implementing a positive, more biblically-oriented patriotism.

A More Excellent Way   At this juncture we shall review some ways of handling the claims of civil religion from a biblical perspective. Admittedly, it is often difficult to determine where patriotism ends and piety begins, but in order to do so, evangelicals must test the rites, symbols, practices and demands of civil religion by biblical truth and Christian history.[18]

First keep in mind that the highest loyalty of a Christian is always to Jesus Christ. A believer's relation to the state is governed by the unshakable conviction that Yahweh God is the absolute sovereign of the universe and that each Christian is subject to the exclusive lordship of Christ. All earthly authority is subordinate to God's authority (Dan. 2:17-45; Jn. 19:10-11; Rom. 13:1). Yahweh is not a local deity whose sole interest is the preservation of any one political society or order. He brings his judgment against sinful rulers and corrupt systems regardless of whether they claim to believe in him or not (Amos 1—2).

Christ has indicated that Christians should render to Caesar that which is Caesar's and to God that which is God's (Mt. 22:17-22). There seems to be little danger that present-day disciples will render unto God what is Caesar's, but there does appear to be a tendency on the part of modern states to demand from Christians what is God's. Although there sometimes are legitimate differences of opinion among Christians over what is God's and what is Caesar's, there is no argument when it comes to worship and sacrifice. That issue clearly involves the lordship of Christ. Should the occasion arise when a choice has to be made between God and country on these matters, the biblical principle is clear: "We must obey God rather than men" (Acts 5:29).

Second, genuine patriotism for the Christian always must be tempered by the knowledge that the fellowship of faith in Christ is not limited by national boundaries (Gal. 3:27-28). The early critics of Christianity coined a phrase intended to discredit the first followers of Jesus—"the third race."[19] As the Romans viewed them the Christians were disloyal to both Greek and Jewish cultures, but the derogatory label was quickly embraced by the Christians because to them it reflected the real nature of their faith. A Christian was a brother or sister no matter who he or she was or whence he or she came. The early believers saw themselves as apart from national or racial classifications.

Third, evangelicals must never forget the scriptural axiom that all men are sinners (Rom. 3:23). Sin is not limited to certain nations, races, cultures or political systems. This truth explains God's purpose for ordaining the existence of governments. God provides sinful people with controls to prevent society from degenerating into total chaos. By the same token, because sinful men govern states, they must always be checked and restrained lest the state become a beast (Rom. 13 and Rev. 13). For the Christian, loyalty to states governed by sinful men is always conditional.

Fourth, a believer in Christ is a nonconformist (Rom. 12:2). Biblical Christians in any society are revolutionaries, for they are out to change the status quo (2 Cor. 5:17). What could be more revolutionary for a Christian in America or in the Soviet Union than to love and feed an enemy (Rom. 12: 20-21)? The manifestation of the fruit of the Spirit in the lives of believers also makes them nonconformists in any culture (Gal. 5:22-23). This scriptural nonconformity has been a part of the Christian heritage and helps explain why most evangelicals in the past seldom were found in the ranks of those who were using religion for purposes of state.

Fifth, a Christian will be a proponent of all that is godly and good. Paul makes it clear that believers are not saved by good works but *for* good works (Eph. 2:8-10). Christians are to be known for their love and peacemaking and their constant offensive against suffering and evil (Rom. 12:20-21; 13:7-8; 2 Cor. 6:6-7).

Sixth and last, evangelical Christians should test the spirits and see if "they are of God" (1 Jn. 4:1). What does the Bible say about a generalized, deistic religion bereft of the language of sin and shorn of the centrality of Christ? The prophet Amos well might respond:

I hate, I despise your feasts,
　　and I take no delight in your solemn assemblies.
Even though you offer me your burnt offerings
　　and cereal offerings,
　　I will not accept them,
and the peace offerings of your fatted beasts
　　I will not look upon.
Take away from me the noise of your songs;
　　to the melody of your harps I will not listen.
But let justice roll down like waters,
　　and righteousness like an everflowing stream.
　　(Amos 5:21-24)

In summary, Christians should preach the gospel, win the lost, teach the gathered saints, minister to the needy, "hate evil, and love good, and establish justice in the gate" (Amos 5:15), and prepare for any eventuality. In order to accomplish this, we challenge every evangelical believer to read the New Testament anew in its entirety in an open-minded, thoughtful and decultured manner. Only then will God have a new opportunity to work through this generation of evangelicals and show them a "more excellent way" (1 Cor. 12:31)!

Suggestions for Positive Patriotism   But can Christians be patriotic Americans and not compromise their faith? Is it possible to resolve the tension which exists and has always existed between genuine biblical Christianity and the state?

Perhaps the place to begin to answer this question is first to define patriotism. By patriotism we mean an expression of love for one's country or native soil which does not demand a loyalty superior to all others. It may be a component of nationalism and it may lead to nationalism, but it is not the same thing as nationalism. Modern nationalism demands the highest loyalty of its adherents, patriotism does not. But even admitting that patriotism does not demand the highest loyalty of a Christian does not resolve that tension between religious and political commitment which, like the poor, will be with us always as long as this present world system continues.[20]

On the other hand there seem to be many in America today who long for a plausible patriotism. Perhaps Christians can help supply a real foundation for a wholesome patriotism based on the common good and positive achievement. Healthy patriotism needs more than the Enlightenment's social contract. It requires hope and a sense of covenant with history. Perhaps evangelicals can exorcise the twin ghosts of the American past from the land—the old Puritan lust for theocracy and the strident, deistic civil millennialism—and then join with other Americans of like mind in building a new patriotism based on honesty and genuine civic virtue.[21]

This brings us to some suggestions for a more positive form

of patriotism among believers. First, a genuine patriot will affirm the past, recognizing that it is a mixture of good and evil. In other words, a Christian's patriotism should be informed and sober, not arrogant and proud. Evangelicals in America should render thanks to God for the positive contributions their country has made to the world at large and for the ideals of freedom and justice it has nurtured and expanded at home. Likewise, repentance is in order for those sinful acts which the nation, its leaders and people have committed. Dr. George Sweeting, president of Moody Bible Institute, catches the sense of this when he affirms: "When America is right, we support her, when America is wrong, we still love her—and do our best to correct her."[22]

Some Christians try to ignore the evils and errors of the past, as though they never existed, while others are so outraged and disillusioned about them that they refuse to believe anything worthwhile resulted from the American experience. Positive patriots, to the contrary, will evaluate the rights and wrongs of our national past in the light of the Bible and dedicate themselves to the task of building a better country where realities will be brought increasingly in alignment with the ideals of the founding documents and our evangelical Christian forebears.

Second, a genuine patriot will affirm the future. This involves not only the confidence that the nation has a future but also that one should be actively engaged in the present to bring about a better tomorrow. This may include openly dissenting from the current practices of the regime and the society that are contrary to the principles of the Bible and national righteousness. For the Christian believer the future is open. Thus, he or she should support those actions which are in keeping with biblical principles and the idealism of the nation's architects, and oppose the ones that are sinful and inhumane. Honest criticism is one of the highest forms of patriotism because it displays faith in the country's ongoing existence and looks for a qualitative improvement in national life that will benefit all citizens.

In this connection we need to point out that the determination to start a new program, build national community and develop some common moral language does not automatically guarantee that the nation will be walking on a path of godliness and righteousness. Such developments could as easily lead to fascism. They do not eliminate evil, bring about personal moral regeneration, make people happy or produce certainty. Only genuine faith in Jesus Christ can do that. This affirmation of the future must be done in a balanced manner, blending realism with idealism and with Christians actively supplying the societal seasoning which Jesus called upon them to do (Mt. 5:13). Only then, perhaps, will the vision of the revolutionary Continental Congress for the new republic be fulfilled—that the American people should beseech God that "vice, prophaneness, extortion, and every evil may be done away... that we may be a reformed and happy people."[23]

Third, a genuine patriot will affirm diversity. To demand conformity to a single party, political ideology, social viewpoint or lifestyle, is hardly in the best interests of a democratic society based on Christian ideals. The United States has had a long tradition of religious pluralism, and since the turn of the century ethnic diversity has been a fact of life as well. This pluralism, although politically and spiritually painful at times, also can be one of America's greatest strengths. Of all people Christians should be able to understand the desire of various ethnic and religious groups to preserve their basic identities in the midst of a strange and sometimes unfriendly world. Moreover, biblical Christianity can bridge real differences between political and ethnic groups and bring genuine healing to the land, if believers will only unleash it. A genuine patriot will take seriously each person as an individual, rather than forcing him or her into an artificial cultural mold. Instead, let God produce "new men and women" through faith in Jesus Christ who are free of cultural hang-ups and who will live to the glory of God no matter in what country they find themselves.

Fourth, a genuine patriot will affirm service. Such an individual will place a high premium on working to solve the country's problems, rather than either seeking scapegoats for them or withdrawing from the political process altogether, lamenting that it is of no use. He or she will accept responsibility for problems, try to discover their sources, hold them up to the light of God's judgment and devote effort to finding solutions. For these patriots the American flag will serve not as a blindfold but as a bright symbol inspiring them to challenge evil at every level of government. This undoubtedly will result in frustrating encounters with structures of self-interest which will yield only reluctantly to pressure. But the effort to bring about changes that benefit a larger section of the populace is most assuredly an act of Christian and patriotic service.

Finally, a genuine patriot will affirm the primacy of God in all of life's relations, political as well as spiritual. As pointed out previously, a Christian's highest allegiance is always to Jesus Christ and all other social and political loyalties must exist in tension with this central fact. There is a clear distinction between showing gratitude and appreciation to the government for performing its duties in a responsible fashion and the idolatrous superpatriotism which regards America or any other country as God's chosen people. Christians can be loyal subjects of almost any state, but their support is always conditional. Nationalistic demands for the ultimate and highest loyalty of the believer must always be rejected. When conflicts arise between the demands of the regime and the will of God, the Christian citizen must become a "prophetic patriot," one who renders loyal protest and faithful dissent.[24]

American Christians who are aware of God's demand for their highest loyalty undoubtedly will be dismayed by the excesses of nationalistic patriotism which they observe around them. That which is frivolously and thoughtlessly exercised in the name of Christ especially will grieve them. Believers have the right, indeed the obligation, to turn the searching, incisive light of the Bible upon their country and its actions even at the risk and cost of being misunderstood and of being labeled unpatriotic by pseudopatriots.

Congressman John B. Anderson, an active evangelical Christian layman, commented incisively on this problem when he participated in a Bicentennial dialog held at Kirkbridge Retreat Center in Pennsylvania in 1975:

> Just as personal love is sometimes blind, so too can love of a country be blind. How many Americans, during our recent Vietnam upheaval, were heard to quote Stephen Decatur: "My country, right or wrong"? "America, love it or leave it," is an example of blind love. "America, improve it or lose it," is responsible, constructive patriotism.[25]

We believe that even in this modern age evangelicals can demonstrate loyalty to their country through the actions of responsible patriotism and loyalty to God through faithful discipleship. In what better way can authentic, positive patriotism be expressed?

A Sober Call to a Devout and Politically Active Life   At this juncture, we hope that many of the questions raised throughout the preceding pages have been answered. We realize that others have not, some because they cannot be. Returning to those serious matters raised at the conclusion of chapter one, what can we say about the future of America in Christian terms? Is evangelical influence in the political life of the nation at an end? Is the intriguing phenomenon of two presidential candidates in 1976 each claiming to have been born again the last gasp of a dying evangelically-oriented America? Are we living in the period of the twilight of the saints?

Obviously, not everyone agrees with our analysis of America as a deeply troubled society. For example, Charles L. Gould, the publisher of the *San Francisco Examiner*, in a 1972 address stressed: "Don't let anyone sell you the idea that ours is a sick society. It is far from perfect, but it is also far and away the most enlightened, most unselfish, most compassionate in the world's history."[26] Many evangelicals would applaud these words, others are not so certain. Carl F. H. Henry is one of those who takes a less optimistic view of the present state of American civilization:

> There are hopeful breakthroughs and sporadic gains at radically secular frontiers, but this is clearly something less than national repentance and renewal. The arena of intellectual and cultural concerns is determinedly non-evangelical. The social and political practices of our time derive less and less inspiration from biblical ideas, and our civilization will not long survive this bankrupting loss. The state of the nation spiritually is generally not good.[27]

We agree with Henry that the spiritual condition of the nation generally is not good. Wishful thinking and the rhetoric of civil religion will not change this fact, because there is simply too much evidence to the contrary. How could a country possessing a level of wealth unparalleled in history permit millions of its citizens to live below the poverty level, while squandering billions of dollars on defense cost overruns and space extravaganzas? In what other place in the world is personal freedom abused and taken so lightly as in America? Where else on earth does the same society on the one hand expend enormous amounts of time and resources trying to preserve and protect life while it condones abortion, capital punishment, war and some forms of euthanasia on the other? What other country has experienced less certainty about crime and how to deal with it in recent years than the United States—from tough programs to break criminal organizations, to the imposition of stringent constitutional restraints upon law enforcement officers, to wrongdoing in high places among "law and order" proponents, to attempts to decriminalize much of what formerly was considered socially and morally wrong. What other nation on earth today is so highly fragmented into so many varied interest and ethnic groups with so little apparent inclination to compromise politically for the common good?[28]

Civil religion merely confuses and compounds these negative features of American society when it calls on us to affirm
faith in a tribal god who blesses our warts as well as our acts
of decency and beauty. Evangelical Christians in other lands
are increasingly vocal in their criticism of civil religion-
ridden Americanism which too often manifests itself in the
activities of otherwise well-meaning Christian missionaries.
Latin American evangelical leader Orlando E. Costas points
out in a recent critique of missionary endeavors originating
in the United States: "[Missionaries from North America] are
part of a syncretistic religious culture. I say syncretistic because many of the values inherent in this culture are defi-
nitely not Christian. Yet they have been made to appear as
if they were."[29]

Many Christian leaders are awakening to the fact that
when Americans preach the gospel, they all too often present
it in a cocoon of American civil religion. Responding to pleas
from his non-American Christian brothers and sisters to reject this perversion of the Christian faith and message, Billy
Graham spoke candidly and pointedly at the 1974 Lausanne
Congress on World Evangelism:

[It is an] error to identify the Gospel with any one particular system or culture. This has been my own danger. When
I go to preach the Gospel, I go as an ambassador for the
Kingdom of God—not America. To tie the Gospel to any
political system, secular program, or society is wrong and
will only serve to divert the Gospel. The Gospel trans-
cends the goals and methods of any political system or any
society, however good it may be.[30]

So we turn once again to the Bible for guidance and help in
this matter of trying to separate the nation—any nation—
from the New Israel of the new covenant—those who have
trusted Jesus Christ as Lord and Savior. Let us reiterate the
reference in the previous chapter to Peter's admonition to
first-century believers: "But you are a chosen race, a royal
priesthood, a holy nation, God's own people, that you may
declare the wonderful deeds of him who called you out of

darkness into his marvelous light" (1 Pet. 2:9). The apostle Paul also reminds us: "For in Christ Jesus you are all sons of God, through faith. For as many of you as were baptized into Christ have put on Christ. There is neither Jew nor Greek, there is neither slave nor free, there is neither male nor female; for you are all one in Christ Jesus" (Gal. 3:26-28).

Evangelicals in the United States need to assess these words in the context of the pressures of civil religion and of the present crisis in American history. The response of evangelicals, both leaders and rank and file, in a large measure will determine the course of events in this country during the next few decades. Ultimately, this may determine whether or not the United States will continue to exist as a democracy beyond the turn of the next century. Christians can no longer afford to adopt an attitude of benign detachment toward the unfolding of events in America. It is a time for action based on biblical truth—before such action becomes irrelevant or impossible. It is time for evangelicals to start living in obedience to God's commands as expressed in Holy Writ. Whether their involvement ultimately makes any difference or not, all believers are expected to be obedient to God's Word. If Christian participation does make a difference, we will be happy, but in any case, followers of Jesus Christ need to be obedient.

It is our considered judgment that there is little hope for the survival of democracy in America and spiritual renewal in the land until Christians start acting like Christians. It is high time that those who claim to be born again get on the right side of the issues and stop supporting the status quo of injustice, racism and oppression of the poor and disinherited. We know that there is room for legitimate differences of opinion among believers on some political problems. But, is there any question where a Christian should stand on the great issues of war and peace, on the politics of human need and compassion, on what to do about corruption in government and the many tawdry people who claim to represent us? Is there any doubt as to what stance Jesus would have us take on the cancer of racism which is a stench in the nostrils of God? Is there any uncertainty about how believers ought to respond to the politics of greed and self-interest, whether at the national or local level? Is there any debate concerning who should be the healers and reconcilers in this spiritually-torn land of ours? Surely not!

If Christians (the real New Testament equivalent of "my people" in 2 Chronicles 7:14) in the United States turn to God in genuine repentance, then there may be hope for the future of America as well as for the preservation of democratic institutions. If believers in this country begin to take a more serious, positive interest in politics, then it may be the dawn of a new day for the gospel of Christ in the United States and the world. If American evangelicals allow their conscience and their political views to be informed by the New Testament, then there well may be a resurgence of the influence of the saints in this country and abroad.

If they do not, then believers probably will continue to be exploited by the state for its own purposes. They will keep on participating in American civil religion with all of its risks and possible harmful effects. The United States, like England of former days, may find itself led astray by calculating politicians who know how to manipulate believers for purposes of the state. It may be like the restoration of Charles II to the throne of England after the failure of the Puritan republican experiment under Cromwell. An eyewitness commented on Charles's return from France in 1660:

> But a cheering multitude were soon streaming down the road to Dover to greet a returning exile, Charles II, who remarked, with his usual wit, when he heard the cheers, that it must have been his own fault that he had been away so long. He then paid his compliments to the rule of the saints by kissing the Bible and describing it as the book he loved best in the world.[31]

Thus one of England's most immoral and egocentric monarchs came home to rule a kingdom which still included large numbers of godly people. But for all practical purposes, the Puritans had lost. It was for them a time of the twilight of the saints.

But it did not have to be then, nor was it permanently true for the English nation. In his own good time, God raised up John Wesley to restore spiritual vigor to that country. God was not yet through with England—ironically, dealing with it next through the Wesleyans rather than the Calvinists. Perhaps in like manner God is not yet finished with the United States.

America is still a country with great potential for good in the world. The nation's political institutions are basically sound, and there is a residual tradition of reform stemming from our Puritan heritage. A large segment of the population has been influenced by the evangelical work ethic and the biblical emphasis on the essential dignity of every individual human being. There are still many Americans of good will who would like this country to become in a real and positive sense a "city upon a hill," an example of decency and humanity to all the world.

But evangelicals must face the agenda for the future with the sober realization that they must confess and renounce the sins of the American past. They must be willing to subject *all* political and economic systems to God's judgment and to test *all* social and political commitments by their fidelity to God's Word. If possible, evangelical leaders representing all parts of the political spectrum need to come together to talk over their differences and hammer out an evangelical consensus. This means putting aside regional and racial prejudice, denominational and theological arrogance, eschatological hobbyhorses and personality conflicts in order to discern the mind of Christ in terms of the pressing social and political problems of modern America. Ideally, it should lead to an agreement on those issues which need to be addressed and on ways which they can be resolved based on principles in harmony with the Bible. In short, Christians in this country need to discuss seriously their differences and do their best to resolve them in the light of the New

Testament which they all claim jointly as the final supreme authoritative guide for followers of Christ.

This is not necessarily to suggest the formation of some kind of evangelical Christian political movement. But it is to imply that a dynamic, holistic faith should produce something more than the immature bickering and extremist political aberrations which today are too often the hallmarks of evangelical Christianity. It is to propose the possibility that a spiritually-virile and biblically-centered evangelical Christianity could supply (as it did in the nineteenth century) American society with the common national values without which a pluralistic nation-state cannot long survive. And we believe this can be done without participating in a compromising, theologically sterile civil religion.[32]

If evangelical Christians—with God's help—cannot agree on some fundamental points of legitimate political involvement and social action, then perhaps America is in the period of the twilight of the saints. If evangelical believers cannot find common ground in Christ, then perhaps the new day will bring some form of fascism to an uninformed, disenchanted, alienated people. Will evangelicals continue to bow to the state in matters of civil religion? Or will they rise to the occasion and meet the future as Senator Hatfield suggests, embracing the power of love and forsaking the love of power.[33]

Is ours then a twilight time of the influence of biblical Christianity in the life of the nation or the threshold of a new day? Only time and the response of present-day Christians will tell.

NOTES

Chapter One

[1]Irving Berlin, "God Bless America," *Best Loved Songs of the American People*, ed. Denes Agay (Garden City, N.Y.: Doubleday, 1975), pp. 341-43.

[2]Richard M. Nixon, *The Presidential Transcripts* (New York: Delacorte Press, 1974), pp. 692-93.

[3]Grant M. Stoltzfus, "Presidential Inaugurations, National Piety, and the God of Christianity," *Gospel Herald*, 66 (Mar. 13, 1973), 221.

[4]"The Voice of God Is Calling," in *The Methodist Hymnal* (Nashville: Methodist Publishing House, 1966), no. 200.

[5]Charles F. Henderson, Jr., "The (Social) Gospel According to 1. Richard Nixon, 2. George McGovern," *Commonweal*, 96 (Sept. 29, 1972), 518-19. Henderson was present at the service.

[6]For examples see Larry Ward, "Love Letter to a Flag," *Christian Crusade*, 40 (Aug. 25, 1974), p. 1; Ernest Toepfer, Jr., "My Flag and Jesus," *Christian Life*, 37 (Nov. 1975), p. 93; Dale Evans Rogers, *Let Freedom Ring!* (Old Tappan, N.J.: Fleming H. Revell, 1975), pp. 11-13; "Factory Worker Suffers Scorn from Flag Display," *Terre Haute Tribune-Star*, Feb. 18, 1973, p. 28; and Richard Mouw, "Long Live (?) the Flag!" *Reformed Journal*, 26 (Sept. 1976), 5.

[7]Patton is an excellent example of the religious and profane merged in the personality of one complex human being. The general could support enthusiastically the work of his chaplains and admonish his troops to rely upon the Almighty, while simultaneously desecrating God's name in almost every sentence he spoke and uttering such unchristian dicta as, "No bastard ever won a war by dying for his country. He won it by making the other poor dumb bastard die for his country." For numerous examples see Ladislas Farago, *Patton: Ordeal and Triumph* (New York: Dell, 1970).

[8]See Jimmy and Carol Owens, *If My People . . .*, Light Records, LS-5657 (1974), with narration by Pat Boone; and Conrad Cherry, ed., *God's New Israel: Religious Interpretations of American Destiny* (Englewood Cliffs, N.J.: Prentice-Hall, 1971). In all fairness it should be noted that the Owenses do, in fact, strive in their popular musical to restrict the definition of God's people to those who trust in Christ, but it is almost inevitable that listeners will not grasp this subtle distinction in the application of 2 Chronicles 7:14.

[9]This definition is our own but we were aided in its formulation by Robert N. Bellah, "Civil Religion in America," *Daedalus*, No. 96 (Winter 1967), pp. 1-21; D. Elton Trueblood, *The Future of the Christian* (New York: Harper & Row, 1971), pp. 83-102; Jürgen Moltmann, "The Cross and Civil Religion," in *Religion and Political Society*, ed. J. Moltmann (New York: Harper & Row, 1974), pp. 9-47; and Will Herberg, "American Civil Religion: What It Is and Whence It Comes," in *American Civil Religion*, ed. Russell E. Richey and Donald G. Jones (New York: Harper & Row, 1974), pp. 76-88.

It is important to keep in mind that the concepts and practices of civil religion rest upon a basic consensus of the majority of the citizens of the state. In other words the majority must give its consent to a minimum body of civic dogma in order for civil religion to be operative and meaningful. Thus, civil religion is dependent upon a national consensus and at the same time lends itself to being structured in a manner to ensure that consensus. This means that American civil religion is a dynamic rather than a static concept. It also means that the American brand of civil religion is a consensus of religious ideas to which the majority of people can give assent in order to live peacefully within society and which the state can utilize to enhance a feeling of national identity and commonality. For a further discussion of this aspect of the subject, see Don S. Ross, "The 'Civil Religion' in America," *Religion in Life*, No. 44 (Spring 1975), pp. 24-35.

[10]Bellah, "Civil Religion in America," p. 1.

[11]Joe McGinniss, *The Selling of the President 1968* (New York: Trident, 1969), p. 193.

[12]The many books on the English Puritans vary widely in quality. Among the best of a number of sound works on the subject are: William Haller, *Liberty and Reformation in the Puritan Revolution* (New York: Harper, 1955); Alan Simpson, *Puritanism in Old and New England* (Chicago: University of Chicago Press, 1955); and Patrick Collinson, *The Elizabethan Puritan Movement* (London: Jonathan Cape, 1966).

[13]John Owen, "Christ's Kingdom and the Magistrate's Power," a sermon published in *The Works of John Owen* (Edinburgh: T. & T. Clark, 1850-53), VIII, 381. For the scriptural basis for Owen's allusion see Jeremiah 8:20.

[14]John Winthrop, *Papers*, ed. A. B. Forbes (Boston: Massachusetts Historical Society, 1929-47), II, 295; and Robert T. Handy, *A Christian America: Protestant Hopes and Historical Realities* (New York: Oxford University Press, 1971), pp. 3-64.

[15]The following historical sketch is based on William L. O'Neill, *Coming Apart: An Informal History of America in the 1960s* (Chicago: Quadrangle, 1971); Yonosuke Nagai, "The United States Is Disintegrating," *Psychology Today*, 6 (May 1972), pp. 24-27, 93-94; David Halberstam, *The Best and the Brightest* (New York: Random House, 1972); Donald W. Harward, ed., *Crisis in Confidence: The Impact of Watergate* (Boston: Little, Brown, 1974); and Jim F. Heath, *Decade of Disillusionment: The Kennedy-Johnson Years* (Bloomington: Indiana University Press, 1975). The loss of a common ideological base for American society is discussed intelligently by John Higham, "Hanging Together: Divergent Unities in American History," *Journal of American History*, No. 61 (June 1974), pp. 5-28.

[16]*Reader's Digest*, 91 (Oct. 1967), pp. 49-54.

[17]Ibid., p. 54.

[18]"Toward the Third Century," *Time*, 107 (Jan. 5, 1976), p. 39.

[19]Periods of spiritual revival and renewal often have accompanied grave political crises. For example, the collapse of medieval civilization came with the Protestant Reformation and a significant revival swept Ulster during the 1920s after the partition of Ireland.

[20]Billy Graham, *The Divine Answer to the National Dilemma* (Manhattan: Kansas State University, 1974), p. 9.

[21]Carl F. H. Henry, "Reflections on a Nation in Transition," *Interpretation*, No. 10 (Jan. 1976), 57.

[22]Barbara W. Tuchman, Foreword to William V. Shannon, *They Could Not Trust the King* (New York: Macmillan, 1974), p. 10.

[23]See note 15 above, also, Daniel Callahan, "The New Pluralism: From Nostalgia to Reality," *Commonweal*, 78 (Sept. 6, 1963), 527-31; and James T. Hickman, "The Polarity of American Evangelicalism," *Religion in Life*, No. 44 (Spring 1975), pp. 47-58.

[24]William G. McLoughlin, ed., *The American Evangelicals, 1800-1900* (New York: Harper & Row, 1968), pp. 1-28.

[25]Halberstam, *The Best and the Brightest*, p. 665. Other assessments of America's recent past and present are equally gloomy. Even the titles reflect the baffled spirit of the times. For instance, see David S. Broder, *The Party's Over: The Failure*

of Politics in America (New York: Harper & Row, 1971); Louis Harris, The Anguish of Change (New York: Norton, 1973); Lewis Lipsitz, ed., The Confused Eagle: Division and Dilemma in American Politics (Boston: Allyn, 1973); David Wise, The Politics of Lying (New York: Random House, 1973); and Jethro Lieberman, How the Government Breaks the Law (Baltimore: Penguin, 1973). See also Stephen V. Monsma, The Unraveling of America (Downers Grove, Ill.: InterVarsity, 1974); and Paul B. Henry, Politics for Evangelicals (Valley Forge, Pa.: Judson, 1974).

[26]"The Spirit of '76," Newsweek, 87 (Jan. 12, 1976), p. 17.

[27]John B. Anderson, Vision and Betrayal in America (Waco: Word, 1975), p. 27.

[28]Carey McWilliams, "Thoughts on the Bicentennial," Nation, 220 (Apr. 12, 1975), 421.

[29]Ibid.

[30]Ibid., p. 423.

[31]For examples, see James C. Longacre, "Mennonites and the Bicentennial," Bicentennial Packet of the Mennonite Central Committee, 1975; James E. Wood, Jr., "Civil Religion and the Bicentennial," Report from the Capital, No. 30 (Oct. 1975), pp. 2, 6; and Joseph H. Jackson, Vernon E. Jordan, Jr., and Larone Bennett, Jr., "Should Blacks Celebrate the Bicentennial?" Ebony, 30 (Aug. 1975), pp. 35-42.

[32]Foy Valentine, "Civil Religion: A Biblical-Theological Assessment," Search, No. 6 (Winter 1976), pp. 47-48.

[33]Francis A. Schaeffer, The Church at the End of the 20th Century (Downers Grove, Ill.: InterVarsity, 1970), pp. 36-37.

[34]The Vietnam War was an example of the lack of consensus among both evangelical Christians and Americans at large. Could the war have been waged without the open and direct support of many important evangelicals in the United States? Why did not a large body of evangelical believers actively oppose the conflict? We seriously doubt that the nation or the American evangelical community can survive another divisive debacle like the Vietnam struggle.

[35]Some readers will take exception to our definition of evangelical—a number claiming that it is too broad and others too narrow. We are aware of the present debate in theological circles over the exact meaning of the term. In many ways it is an elusive label. In recent years it has been appropriated by theologically conservative Protestants who want to distinguish themselves from "fundamentalists" because of their desire to expand their relationships with other Christians and to assume a greater responsibility for society and culture at large. Others simply do not want to be associated with sociological fundamentalism even though they agree with its basic theology. In this work we are endeavoring to use the term in its wider, more historic meaning. Thus, we would include under the rubric such apparently diverse groups as theological fundamentalists, those in the Anabaptist tradition who may be reluctant to advocate full participation in the sinful society of the world-at-large, Calvinists who put more emphasis on a covenantal than an experiential faith, confessional Lutherans who adhere stoutly to their founder's stress on law and gospel, Wesleyans of all stripes who share in the social impulse which has so characterized the movement throughout its history, and even some Roman Catholic and Eastern Orthodox Christians who place the authority of church tradition alongside that of Scripture but yet recognize the importance of the "new birth." As a matter of fact the authors of this volume themselves represent two different strands of present-day evangelical Christianity but find no trouble in embracing in common the basic doctrines of the historic faith. Finally, we are aware of the historical problem that seventeenth-century Christians probably would not define themselves in exactly the same terms as twentieth-century evangelicals. But we believe that the categories we set

forth apply to them with reasonable accuracy. For a more detailed discussion of evangelical theology and the present-day problem of evangelical identity, see Carl F. H. Henry, ed., *Basic Christian Doctrines* (New York: Holt, Rinehart, and Winston, 1962); David F. Wells and John D. Woodbridge, eds., *The Evangelicals* (rev. ed., Grand Rapids: Baker, 1977); Hickman, "The Polarity in American Evangelicalism," pp. 47-58; Richard Quebedeaux, "The Evangelicals: New Trends and New Tensions," *Christianity and Crisis*, 36 (Sept. 20, 1976), 197-202; and Carl F. H. Henry, *Evangelicals in Search of Identity* (Waco: Word, 1976).

Chapter Two

[1]G. K. Chesterton, "What I Saw in America," in *The Man Who Was Chesterton,* ed. Raymond T. Bond (New York: Dodd, Mead, 1946), p. 235.

[2]Ibid., p. 192. Mead's essay originally appeared in *Church History*, No. 36 (Sept. 1967), pp. 1-22, and is reprinted in a collection of his works, see Sidney E. Mead, *The Nation With the Soul of a Church* (New York: Harper & Row, 1975), pp. 48-77.

[3]Chesterton, "What I Saw in America," p. 188.

[4]Ibid., p. 189.

[5]For a brief historical analysis of civil religion see Robert D. Linder, "Civil Religion in Historical Perspective: The Reality That Underlies the Concept," *Journal of Church and State*, 17 (Autumn 1975), 399-421.

[6]Alfred Cobban, *In Search of Humanity* (New York: Braziller, 1960); and Peter Gay, *The Enlightenment: An Interpretation* (New York: Knopf, 1966-69), 2 vols. Also deserving of another look, especially in the light of the renewed interest in the study of civil religion, is Carl Becker's highly suggestive *The Heavenly City of the Eighteenth-Century Philosophers* (New Haven: Yale University Press, 1932).

[7]For several views on Rousseau and his consistency or lack thereof, see C. E. Vaughan, ed., *The Political Writings of Jean-Jacques Rousseau* (Cambridge: University Press, 1935), 2 vols., esp. Vaughan's introduction; David Cameron, "Rousseau, Professor Derathé and Natural Law," *Political Studies*, 20 (June 1972), 195-201; and Maurice W. Cranston and Richard S. Peters, ed., *Hobbes and Rousseau: A Collection of Critical Essays* (Garden City, N.Y.: Doubleday, 1972).

[8]Jean-Jacques Rousseau, *The Social Contract and Discourses*, ed. G. D. H. Cole (New York: Dutton, 1950), p. 139. Also see Jean-Jacques Rousseau, *Oeuvres Complètes, Du Contrat Social*, ed. Bernard Gagnebin and Marcel Raymond (Paris: Gallimard, 1964), III, 468.

[9]In Rousseau's social contract each individual voluntarily forms part of what he calls "the general will." Because each person forms part of the whole, they continue to remain free. However, Rousseau also argues that the majority, which always knows what is best for the group, is the custodian of the general will. The individual must obey the general will, for the majority is a better judge than the individual of what is best for him. On this topic see Rousseau, *Du Contrat Social*, pp. 368-75.

[10]Louis J. Voskuil, "Jean-Jacques Rousseau: Secular Salvation and Civil Religion," *Fides et Historia*, No. 7 (Spring 1975), pp. 11-26.

[11]This brief summary of Rousseau's concept of civil religion and its relation to the totality of his discussion of the social contract does not do full justice to Rousseau. For one thing, his fear that the body politic as a whole might manifest many of the same selfish characteristics as its individual component parts enters in here. It may be that civil religion was a device designed to pick up any loose ends that might be left over after his treatment of the relationship between individual selfishness and social obligation. Thus, some students of Rousseau feel that there is a transcendent element in Rousseau's civil faith, but it certainly is not the per-

sonal God of Christianity. Moreover, it would appear that a deistic civil faith in a pluralistic and secular modern state would find it difficult to resist the state becoming the transcendent point of reference for the civic faith of its adherents. For example, see Waldemar Gurian, "Totalitarianism as Political Religion," in *Totalitarianism*, ed. Carl J. Friedrich (Cambridge: Harvard University Press, 1954), pp. 119-29; and Reinhold Niebuhr, *Christianity and Power Politics* (New York: Scribner's, 1940), pp. 117-30. Compare Ps. 9 and Is. 2:1-4.

[12]Rousseau, *Du Contrat Social*, pp. 464-68.

[13]Émile Durkheim, *The Elementary Forms of the Religious Life* (New York: Free Press, 1965), pp. 474-75.

[14]Rousseau, *Du Contrat Social*, p. 468; and Plato, *The Dialogues*, ed. Benjamin Jowett (Oxford: Oxford University Press, 1892), II, 109-29.

[15]Plato, *The Republic*, ed. Benjamin Jowett (Oxford: Oxford University Press, 1892), I, 621-82. See also Ellis Sandoz, "The Civil Theology of Liberal Democracy: Locke and His Predecessors," *Journal of Politics*, No. 34 (Feb. 1972), pp. 2-7.

[16]Michael A. Smith, *From Christ to Constantine* (London: Inter-Varsity, 1971), pp. 74-91. Also see Ethelbert Stauffer, *Christ and the Caesars* (London: SCM, 1955); and A. N. Sherwin-White, *Roman Society and Roman Law in the New Testament* (Oxford: Clarendon Press, 1963).

[17]Edward Gibbon, *The History of the Decline and Fall of the Roman Empire*, ed. J. B. Bury (New York: F. De Fau, 1906), I, 35-36.

[18]Eusebius of Caesarea, *The Ecclesiastical History* (Cambridge: Harvard University Press, 1953-57), I, 405-37; John R. Knipfing, "The Libelli of the Decian Persecution," *Harvard Theological Review*, 16 (Oct. 1923), 345-90; and Stauffer, *Christ and the Caesars*, pp. 205-63.

[19]J. W. C. Wand, *A History of the Early Church to A.D. 500* (London: Methuen, 1937), p. 131; and Guglielmo Ferrero and Corrado Barbagallo, *A Short History of Rome* (New York: Putnam's, 1918-19), II, 418.

[20]Ernest Barker, *Church, State and Education* (Ann Arbor: University of Michigan Press, 1957), pp. 131-35.

[21]Ernst H. Kantorowicz, "Pro Patria Mori in Medieval Political Thought," *American Historical Review*, 56 (Apr. 1951), 472-92.

[22]Joseph R. Strayer, "Problems of State-Building," in *Medieval Statecraft and the Perspectives of History*, ed. J. Strayer (Princeton: Princeton University Press, 1971), pp. 251-348.

[23]J. E. J. Quicherat, *Procès de condamnation et de rehabilitation de Jeanne d'Arc* (Paris: Renouard, 1841-49), V, 127.

[24]Gerhart B. Ladner, "Aspects of Medieval Thought on Church and State," *Review of Politics*, 9 (Oct. 1947), 403-22.

[25]Kantorowicz, "Pro Patria Mori in Medieval Thought," p. 491.

[26]G. R. Cragg, *The Church and the Age of Reason, 1648-1789* (Baltimore: Penguin, 1970), pp. 209-33.

[27]Ronald J. VanderMolen, "Western Secularization as a Continuing Process: Ironic Origins and Puzzling Results," *Fides et Historia*, No. 8 (Fall 1975), pp. 50-51.

[28]David J. Diephouse, "The 'German Catastrophe' Revisited: Civil Religion in the Third Reich," *Fides et Historia*, No. 7 (Spring 1975), p. 55.

[29]Reinhold Niebuhr, *Christianity and Power Politics*, pp. 117-30; and Jacques Ellul, "Les religions séculières," *Foi et Vie*, No. 69 (1970), p. 73.

[30]John Aylmer, *An Harborowe for Faithfull and Trewe Subjects* (Strassburg: n.p., 1559), sig. P4, margin; sig. R.

[31]John Foxe, *The Acts and Monuments*, ed. S. R. Cattley, 1837-41 (rpt. New York:

AMS Press, 1965), I, vi-viii, 305-86, *et passim.*

[32]William Haller, *Foxe's Book of Martyrs and the Elect Nation* (London: Jonathan Cape, 1963), pp. 224-50; and William M. Lamont, *Godly Rule: Politics and Religion, 1603-1660* (New York: St. Martin's, 1969).

[33]Bruce Murphy, "Christianity and Civil Religion in Cromwellian England," *Fides et Historia,* No. 7 (Spring 1975), pp. 27-39.

[34]Owen, "Christ's Kingdom and the Magistrate's Power," p. 381.

[35]Sandoz, "The Civil Theology of Liberal Democracy," pp. 9-14, 34-35.

[36]George F. Willison, *Saints and Strangers* (New York: Reynal & Hitchcock, 1945), see esp. pp. 1-11, 121-68, and 408-22.

[37]B. P. Poore, ed., *The Federal and State Constitutions* (Washington: USGPO, 1878), I, 931.

[38]William Bradford, *Of Plymouth Plantation, 1620-1647,* ed. S. E. Morison (New York: Knopf, 1952).

[39]Winthrop, *Papers,* II, 29; and Loren Baritz, *City on a Hill: A History of Ideas and Myths in America* (New York: Wiley, 1964), pp. 3-45.

[40]For example, see John Adams to Hezekiah Niles, Feb. 13, 1818, in *The Selected Writings of John and John Quincy Adams,* ed. Adrienne Koch and William Peden (New York: Knopf, 1946), p. 203; Catherine L. Albanese, *Sons of the Fathers: The Civil Religion of the American Revolution* (Philadelphia: Temple University Press, 1976); and Sydney E. Ahlstrom, "Religion, Revolution and the Rise of Modern Nationalism: Reflections on the American Experience," *Church History,* 44 (Dec. 1975), 499-500.

[41]John E. Smylie, "National Ethos and the Church," *Theology Today,* 20 (Oct. 1963), 313-18; Conrad Cherry, "Two American Sacred Ceremonies: Their Implications for the Study of Religion in America," *American Quarterly,* 21 (Winter 1969), 739-54; and Sacvan Bercovitch, *The Puritan Origins of the American Self* (New Haven: Yale University Press, 1975).

[42]Thaddeus Fiske, *A Sermon, Delivered Dec. 29, 1799, At the Second Parish in Cambridge, Being the Lord's Day, Immediately Following the Melancholy Intelligence of the Death of General George Washington, Late President of the United States of America* (Boston: James Cutler, 1800), p. 10. Also see Robert P. Hay, "George Washington: American Moses," *American Quarterly,* 21 (Winter 1969), 780-91. Interestingly, as a deist Washington was hardly given to seeing God's hand in history, not to mention regarding himself as directly commissioned by Yahweh to be the Moses of the New World. Particularly helpful is Paul F. Boller, *George Washington and Religion* (Dallas: Southern Methodist University Press, 1963).

[43]United States President, *Inaugural Addresses of the Presidents of the United States From George Washington, 1789 to Richard Milhous Nixon, 1973* (Washington: USGPO, 1974), p. 21.

[44]Bellah, "Civil Religion in America," pp. 7-9; and Trueblood, *The Future of the Christian,* pp. 89-92. Later, in its more debased form, American civil religion also embraced the concept of the president as high priest of the national faith, a motif discussed in some detail in chapter three.

[45]Conrad Cherry, "Two American Sacred Ceremonies," p. 741. Also see William L. Warner, *American Life: Dream and Reality* (Chicago: University of Chicago Press, 1957).

[46]Some recently have argued with considerable cogency that since the 1950s professional football has replaced the public schools as the chief vehicle for propagating and celebrating the ideals of American civil religion. For example, see Richard T. Hughes, "The New Expression of the American Civil Religion," *Mis-*

sion, 6 (April 1973), 291-94; and Perry C. Cotham, *Politics, Americanism, and Christianity* (Grand Rapids: Baker, 1976), pp. 259-67.

[47] Cherry, "Two American Sacred Ceremonies," pp. 739-54; Bellah, "Civil Religion in America," p. 11; and Trueblood, *The Future of the Christian*, pp. 98-99. It is noteworthy that the Lincoln Memorial provided the setting for both Martin Luther King, Jr.'s "I Have a Dream" speech on August 28, 1963, and Billy Graham's Honor America Day address on July 4, 1970.

[48] Oliver Wendell Holmes, *The Poetical Works of Oliver Wendell Holmes* (Boston: Houghton Mifflin, 1975), p. 194. The "prophets of Baal" and the villains of Holmes's piece are, of course, the seceding Southerners. Ironically, many Southern evangelicals today are fond of citing this poem as an act of patriotic piety.

[49] Nathan O. Hatch, "The Origins of Civil Millennialism in America: New England Clergymen, War with France, and the Revolution," *William and Mary Quarterly*, 31 (July 1974), 429. See also Nathan O. Hatch, *The Sacred Cause of Liberty: Millennial Thought in Revolutionary New England* (New Haven: Yale University Press, 1977); Robert G. Clouse, *Millennialism and America* (Portland, Ore.: Western Baptist Press, 1977); and M. Darrol Bryant, "America as God's Kingdom," in Moltmann, *Religion and Political Society*, pp. 54-94.

[50] Smylie, "National Ethos and the Church," p. 314.

[51] *New York Morning News*, Dec. 27, 1845, quoted in Frederick Merk, *Manifest Destiny and Mission in American History* (New York: Knopf, 1963), p. 32.

[52] Matthew Simpson, "Indiana Conference," *The Methodist*, 2 (Oct. 12, 1861), 313. Also see James E. Kirby, "Matthew Simpson and the Mission of America," *Church History*, 36 (Sept. 1967), 299-307.

[53] McLoughlin, *The American Evangelicals*, p. 1. Also see Higham, "Hanging Together," pp. 11-13.

[54] Carlton J. H. Hayes, *Essays on Nationalism* (New York: Macmillan, 1926), p. 6 *et passim*.

[55] 2nd ed. (New York: Ronald Press, 1956), ch. 3. Also see Ahlstrom, "Religion, Revolution and the Rise of Modern Nationalism"; and Sherwood E. Wirt, "Calvin's Influence in America," *Christianity Today*, 20 (Oct. 24, 1975), pp. 4-6.

[56] For a first-rate discussion of this subject see Robert W. Lynn, "Civil Catechetics in Mid-Victorian America: Some Notes About American Civil Religion, Past and Present," *Religious Education*, No. 48 (Jan.-Feb. 1973), pp. 5-27.

[57] Henry May, *The Enlightenment in America* (New York: Oxford University Press, 1977).

[58] See Ralph H. Gabriel, *The Course of American Democratic Thought*, 2nd ed. (New York: Ronald Press, 1956), pp. 14-25, 33-38; Mead, *The Nation With the Soul of a Church*, pp. 56-57; Ahlstrom, "Religion, Revolution and the Rise of Modern Nationalism," pp. 502-03; and Seymour M. Lipset, *The First New Nation* (New York: Basic Books, 1963), pp. 61-98.

[59] Sydney E. Ahlstrom, "Requiem for Patriotic Piety," *Worldview*, No. 18 (Aug. 1972), pp. 9-11; and Trueblood, *The Future of the Christian*, pp. 88-89. For the Bismarck comment, see Thomas A. Bailey, *The American Pageant* (Lexington, Mass.: D. C. Heath, 1971), p. 668; and John Bartlett, *Familiar Quotations* (Boston: Little, Brown, 1955), p. 1008A.

[60] Aaron I. Abell, *The Urban Impact on American Protestantism, 1865-1900* (Cambridge: Harvard University Press, 1943); Sidney E. Mead, *The Lively Experiment: The Shaping of Christianity in America* (New York: Harper & Row, 1963), esp. pp. 134-55; Sydney E. Ahlstrom, *A Religious History of the American People* (New Haven: Yale University Press, 1972), pp. 842-56; and Ross, "The 'Civil Religion' in America," pp. 33-35.

Chapter Three

[1]The indispensable source for information on the religious support of the American war effort is Ray H. Abrams, *Preachers Present Arms* (1933; rpt. with two additional chapters by the author, Scottdale, Pa.: Herald Press, 1968).

[2]Ibid., p. 55.

[3]*Congressional Record*, Vol. 56, Pt. 1 (Jan. 10, 1918), 762.

[4]Abrams, *Preachers Present Arms*, pp. 110-11.

[5]John E. Wickham (Superior of the New York Apostolic Fathers), "Christmas Sermon," *New York Times*, Dec. 26, 1917, p. 3; and James I. Vance (Minister of the First Presbyterian Church, Nashville), "What Is Patriotism?" *Christian Century*, No. 34 (Sept. 20, 1917), p. 10.

[6]Abrams, *Preachers Present Arms*, p. 124.

[7]George M. Marsden, "From Fundamentalism to Evangelicalism: A Historical Analysis," in Wells and Woodbridge, *The Evangelicals*, pp. 124-44.

[8]Quoted in Dorothy Dohen, *Nationalism and American Catholicism* (New York: Sheed & Ward, 1967), pp. 147-48.

[9]Quoted in Abrams, *Preachers Present Arms*, p. 86.

[10]Text of letter included in Theodore Roosevelt, *The Great Adventure* (New York: Scribners, 1918), pp. 203-04.

[11]Ahlstrom, *Religious History of the American People*, pp. 898-99.

[12]Eldon G. Ernst, *Moment of Truth for Protestant America: Interchurch Campaigns Following World War One* (Missoula, Mont.: Scholars' Press, 1974).

[13]Ahlstrom, *Religious History of the American People*, p. 899.

[14]Robert D. Linder, "The Resurgence of Evangelical Social Concern (1925-75)," in Wells and Woodbridge, *The Evangelicals*, pp. 211-20, summarizes the impact of the developments of the 1920s on evangelical Christianity. See also Linder, "Fifty Years After Scopes: Lessons to Learn, a Heritage to Reclaim," *Christianity Today*, 19 (July 18, 1975), pp. 7-10; and Ferenc M. Szasz, "The Progressive Clergy and the Kingdom of God," *Mid-America*, No. 55 (Jan. 1973), pp. 3-20.

[15]Ahlstrom, *Religious History of the American People*, p. 915.

[16]Linder, "Resurgence," p. 219.

[17]Ahlstrom, *Religious History of the American People*, p. 915.

[18]Ahlstrom, "Requiem for Patriotic Piety," pp. 10-11.

[19]Merlin Gustafson, "President Hoover and the National Religion," *Journal of Church and State*, No. 16 (Winter 1974), p. 85. See also Paul A. Carter, *The Decline and Revival of the Social Gospel: Social and Political Liberalism in American Protestant Churches, 1920-1940* (Ithaca: Cornell University Press, 1956).

[20]For example, only 8 Catholics were numbered among 214 federal judges appointed by Harding, Coolidge and Hoover, while 51 of the 196 judicial appointments made by Roosevelt were Catholics. Samuel Lubell, *The Future of American Politics* (New York: Harper & Row, 1952), p. 78.

[21]Calvin Coolidge, *The Autobiography of Calvin Coolidge* (New York: Cosmopolitan, 1929), pp. 175, 178.

[22]Ibid., p. 235.

[23]*New York Times*, Mar. 5, 1925, p. 2.

[24]Samuel I. Rosenman, *Working with Roosevelt* (New York: Harper, 1952), p. 433.

[25]*New York Times*, Jan. 5, 1939, p. 12.

[26]*New York Times*, Jan. 7, 1941, p. 1.

[27]*New York Times*, Dec. 9, 1941, p. 1.

[28]*New York Times*, Jan. 7, 1942, p. 1.

[29]*New York Times*, June 7, 1944, p. 1.

[30]*New York Times*, Mar. 27, 1943, p. 7; and *Time*, 44 (Dec. 12, 1944), p. 73.

[31]*New York Times*, May 22, 1944, p. 9; and Frances Brentano, ed., *Nation Under God* (Great Neck, N.Y.: Channel Press, 1957), p. 92.

[32]*New York Times*, Apr. 17, 1945, p. 12.

[33]*New York Times*, Jan. 21, 1949, p. 4.

[34]Quoted in *Christian Century*, 67 (June 8, 1950), 782.

[35]*Public Papers of the Presidents of the United States. Harry S. Truman, 1951* (Washington, USGPO, 1965), pp. 211-12.

[36]Douglas MacArthur, *Revitalizing a Nation* (Chicago: Heritage Foundation, 1952), pp. 18-20.

[37]Edward L. R. Elson, *America's Spiritual Recovery* (Westwood, N.J.: Revell, 1954), p. 44. See also Harvey G. Cox, *Military Chaplains: From a Religious Military to a Military Religion* (New York: American Report Press, 1971).

[38]Merlin Gustafson, "Church, State, and the Cold War, 1945-1952," *Journal of Church and State*, No. 8 (Winter 1966), pp. 49-63.

[39]*New York Times*, May 23, 1954, p. 7; June 15, 1954, p. 31. See also Gerard Kaye and Ferenc M. Szasz, "Adding 'Under God' to the Pledge of Allegiance," *Encounter*, No. 34 (1973), 52-56. This development is traced in more detail in Richard V. Pierard, "One Nation Under God—Judgment or Jingoism?" *Studies in Christian Social Ethics*, ed. Perry C. Cotham (Grand Rapids: Baker, 1978).

[40]Merlin Gustafson, "The Religion of a President," *Christian Century*, 86 (Apr. 30, 1969), 610-13.

[41]Bela Kornitzer, *The Great American Heritage* (New York: Farrar, Straus, & Cudahy, 1955), p. 137; "Dwight D. Eisenhower's Bible-Based Legacy," *Bible Society Record*, 114 (July-Aug., 1969); and Mead, *The Nation With the Soul of a Church*, p. 25.

[42]*New York Times*, Jan. 21, 1953, p. 9; and Elson, *America's Spiritual Recovery*, pp. 53-55.

[43]*America*, 88 (Mar. 9, 1953), 612.

[44]James DeForest Murch, *Cooperation Without Compromise* (Grand Rapids: Eerdmans, 1956), pp. 150-51.

[45]*New York Times*, July 10, 1953, p. 6.

[46]*Congressional Record*, Vol. 99, Pt. 9 (Feb. 10, 1953), A573.

[47]*Vital Speeches of the Day*, 20 (Aug. 15, 1954), 642. The address was delivered in Washington on July 25, 1954.

[48]William Lee Miller, *Piety Along the Potomac: Notes on Politics and Morals in the Fifties* (Boston: Houghton Mifflin, 1964), pp. 19-20, 34; and *New York Times*, Dec. 23, 1952, p. 16.

[49]Merlin Gustafson, "The Religious Role of the President," *Midwest Journal of Political Science*, 14 (Nov. 1970), 712; and Charles P. Henderson, Jr., *The Nixon Theology* (New York: Harper & Row, 1972), p. 26. See also Paul A. Carter, "The Pastoral Office of the President," *Theology Today*, No. 25 (Apr. 1968), pp. 52-63.

[50]*Christian Century*, 90 (May 16, 1973), 555.

[51]Bernard F. Donahue, "The Political Use of Religious Symbols," *Review of Politics*, No. 37 (Jan. 1975), pp. 60-61.

[52]Theodore C. Sorenson, *Kennedy* (New York: Harper & Row, 1965), p. 19.

[53]Bellah, "Civil Religion in America," pp. 1-5. For a compilation of Kennedy's statements on religion see Nicholas A. Schneider, ed., *Religious Views of President John F. Kennedy* (St. Louis: Herder, 1965).

[54]Bellah, "Civil Religion in America," p. 15.

[55]*West Virginia Board of Education* v. *Barnette* 319 U.S. 642 (1943).

[56]For a thorough discussion of these cases and their implications for Christians see Donald E. Pitzer, "Christianity in the Public Schools," in *Protest and Politics:*

Christianity and Contemporary Affairs, ed. Robert G. Clouse, Robert D. Linder and Richard V. Pierard (Greenwood, S.C.: Attic Press, 1968), pp. 151-81.

[57]*New York Times*, June 28, 1962, p. 14.

[58]Billy Graham, "Our Right to Require Belief," *Saturday Evening Post*, 235 (Feb. 17, 1962), p. 8.

[59]Speech entitled "Our National Relationship to God: The Threat of Secularism," delivered before the Americanism Forum in Houston, Jan. 25, 1964. Published in *Vital Speeches of the Day*, 30 (Apr. 1, 1964), 357.

[60]Quoted in *Congressional Record*, Vol. 110, Pt. 4 (March 10, 1964), 4799.

[61]Text as printed in *Christian Century*, 81 (Apr. 15, 1964), 475. A most thoughtful assessment of the problem is Harman R. Clark, Jr., "I'm Against Prayer in Schools," *Moody Monthly*, 77 (Oct. 1976), pp. 70-72.

[62]Richard J. Neuhaus, *Time Toward Home: The American Experience As Revelation* (New York: Seabury, 1975), p. 19.

[63]Paul Goodman, *Growing Up Absurd* (New York: Random House, 1969), p. 97.

[64]Bill Adler, ed., *The Wit and Wisdom of Billy Graham* (New York: Random House, 1967), pp. 94-95, 81.

[65]Dwight D. Eisenhower, "Let's Close Ranks on the Home Front," *Reader's Digest*, 92 (Apr. 1968), pp. 49-53.

[66]*Rocky Mountain News* (Denver), Aug. 25, 1965, p. 5. A year later Graham in more subdued fashion referred to the war as "the battle of the world" and said "the stakes are extremely high for the Western world." *New York Times*, Dec. 29, 1966, p. 2. When the *Christian Century* accused him of giving "the war the blessing of the gospel from coast to coast" and condoning "the killing, maiming, and burning as indispensable to the victory of a great Christian cause," Graham retorted that he had been "extremely careful" not to be drawn into the "moral implications" or "tactical military problems" of the conflict. *Christian Century*, 84 (Jan. 25, 1967), 100; 84 (Mar. 29, 1967), 411.

[67]*New York Times*, Dec. 25, 1966, p. 3; Dec. 27, 1966, p. 4.

[68]Mark O. Hatfield, *Between a Rock and a Hard Place* (Waco: Word, 1976), pp. 94-99.

[69]James Deakin, "The Dark Side of L.B.J.," *Esquire*, 68 (Aug. 1967), pp. 45-48, 134-36; and *New York Times*, Jan. 21, 1965, p. 17.

[70]Henderson, *Nixon Theology*, pp. 3-7. This is an interesting although undocumented source of information about his religious views. Unfortunately, it appeared too soon to take into account the Watergate revelations.

[71]Ben Hibbs, ed., *White House Sermons* (New York: Harper & Row, 1972). contains the texts of the sermons and prayers given at these services during the first three years of the Nixon Administration. A helpful critique is Reinhold Niebuhr, "The King's Chapel and the King's Court," *Christianity and Crisis*, 29 (Aug. 4, 1969), 211-12.

[72]Jeb Stuart Magruder in an interview with Studs Terkel, "Reflections on a Course in Ethics," *Harpers*, 247 (Oct. 1973), 70; and Wallace Henley, *The White House Mystique* (Old Tappan, N.J.: Revell, 1976), pp. 66-67.

[73]Henderson, *Nixon Theology*, p. 41.

[74]Richard V. Pierard, "Can Billy Graham Survive Richard Nixon?" *Reformed Journal*, No. 24 (Apr. 1974), pp. 7-13.

[75]Henley, *White House Mystique*, p. 74.

[76]For example, in the opening paragraph of the first chapter of *WASHINGTON: Christians in the Corridors of Power*, the authors lead off with the unequivocal assertion: "President Gerald Ford is a Christian, an acknowledged follower of Jesus Christ." James C. Hefley and Edward E. Plowman, *WASHINGTON: Chris-*

tians in the Corridors of Power (Wheaton: Tyndale, 1975), p. 13.

[77]Henry, "Reflections on a Nation in Transition," p. 56; and "The Evangelical Vote," *Newsweek*, 80 (Oct. 30, 1972), p. 93.

[78]*Public Papers of the Presidents of the United States. Richard Nixon, 1970* (Washington: USGPO, 1971), p. 16.

[79]Ibid., 1973 (Washington: USGPO, 1975), p. 15.

[80]Jeb Stuart Magruder, *An American Life: One Man's Road to Watergate* (New York: Atheneum, 1974), pp. 119-21.

[81]*New York Times*, Feb. 1, 1974, p. 10.

[82]*New Republic*, 173 (Nov. 22, 1975), 31.

[83]Cotham, *Politics*, pp. 148-49.

[84]*Public Papers of the Presidents of the United States. Gerald R. Ford, 1974* (Washington: USGPO, 1975), p. 2.

[85]Ibid., pp. 101-03.

Chapter Four

[1]*Vision and Betrayal*, pp. 55-56. Anderson is an active evangelical churchman and a member of the Republican leadership in the U.S. House of Representatives.

[2]Carlton J. H. Hayes delineates the factors making up a nation in his classic work, *Essays on Nationalism*, (1926; rpt. New York: Russell and Russell, 1966), ch. 1. He stresses commonality as the key to nationhood. In other words a viable nation will hold the majority (the more, the better) of the following in common: territory, allegiance to certain accepted political institutions, religion, language, ethnic descent, customs and traditions.

[3]Bellah, "Civil Religion in America," pp. 4, 18.

[4]Mead, *The Nation With the Soul of a Church*, pp. 60-76.

[5]Smylie, "National Ethos and the Church," pp. 313-21.

[6]Cotham, *Politics*, pp. 160-61.

[7]Robert N. Bellah, *Beyond Belief: Essays on Religion in a Post-Traditional World* (New York: Harper & Row, 1970), p. 168. Also see Michael Novak, *Choosing Our King: Powerful Symbols in Presidential Politics* (New York: Macmillan, 1974), pp. 143-44.

[8]Mimeographed sermon, "This Nation Under God," July 4, 1976, p. 3. Copy in possession of the authors.

[9]Tracy Early, "Churches of the Revolution: The Cause of Justice," *Christian Herald*, No. 99 (July-Aug. 1976), p. 8; and Robert Benne and Philip Hefner, *Defining America: A Christian Critique of the American Dream* (Philadelphia: Fortress, 1974), pp. 117-18.

[10]Neal Riemer, "The Civil Religion in America and Prophetic Politics," *The Drew Gateway*, No. 44 (Fall 1972), p. 21.

[11]Sermon of July 4, 1976, The Lutheran Hour, Oswald Hoffmann, *Under God* (St. Louis: International Lutheran Laymen's League, 1976), p. 2.

[12]Alfred Balitzer, "Some Thoughts About Civil Religion," *Journal of Church and State*, No. 16 (Winter 1974), pp. 33-34.

[13]Mead, *The Nation With the Soul of a Church*, p. 65.

[14]Novak, *Choosing Our King*, p. 128; and Benne and Hefner, *Defining America*, p. 117.

[15]Novak, *Choosing Our King*, p. 118; Martin E. Marty, "Two Kinds of Two Kinds of Civil Religion," in Richey and Jones, *American Civil Religion*, pp. 139-57; and Marty, *A Nation of Behavers* (Chicago: University of Chicago Press, 1976), pp. 180-203.

[16]*Congressional Record*, Vol. 119, Pt. 33 (Dec. 20, 1973), 42669-70.

[17]Ibid., pp. 42670-71.

[18]The full text of the two-hour proceeding is contained in Ibid., Vol. 120, Pt. 9 (Apr. 30, 1974), 12270-81. See also *Christianity Today*, 18 (May 24, 1974), pp. 50-51.

[19]*Congressional Record*, Vol. 120, Pt. 9 (Apr. 30, 1974), 12271-72.

[20]Ibid., p. 12272.

[21]Ibid., pp. 12274-75.

[22]Ibid., pp. 12274, 12276.

[23]John A. Mackay, *Heritage and Destiny* (New York: Macmillan, 1943), pp. 82-103.

[24]Robert N. Bellah, *The Broken Covenant* (New York: Seabury, 1975). In his chapter "The Revolution and the Civil Religion," *Religion and the American Revolution*, ed. Jerald C. Brauer (Philadelphia: Fortress, 1976), pp. 55-73, Bellah maintains that the founders of the republic identified civil religion with "virtue," that is, concern for the common good, but during the ensuing years an emphasis on self-interest and utilitarianism pulled it down from its lofty moral heights.

[25]Bellah, "Civil Religion in America," p. 16; and Bellah, *The Broken Covenant*, p. 1.

[26]New York: Seabury, 1975.

[27]Ibid., pp. 128, 169.

[28]Richard J. Neuhaus, "Patriotism and Puritans," *Worldview*, 21 (Dec. 1975), 5.

[29]Merrill R. Abbey, *Day Dawns in Fire: America's Quest for Meaning* (Philadelphia: Fortress, 1976), pp. 22-24; and John B. Anderson, "Christians Must Fill Nation's Spiritual Void," *The Evangelical Beacon*, Nov. 26, 1974, p. 11. Anderson's words were echoed by presidential contender Ronald Reagan at the Republican National Convention in Kansas City, in August 1976, *Kansas City Times*, Aug. 20, 1976, p. 4B.

[30]Bellah, *The Broken Covenant*, pp. 50-52.

[31]Trueblood, *The Future of the Christian*, pp. 89, 96.

[32]*Inaugural Addresses of the Presidents*, p. 128.

[33]Sam Keen and Robert Bellah, "Civil Religion: The Sacred and the Political in American Life," *Psychology Today*, 9 (Jan. 1976), p. 58.

[34]Text printed in Leon Friedman, *The Civil Rights Reader: Basic Documents of the Civil Rights Movement* (New York: Walker, 1968), pp. 110-13.

[35]*Public Papers of the Presidents of the United States. John F. Kennedy, 1963* (Washington: USGPO, 1964), pp. 469-70.

[36]*New York Times*, Mar. 25, 1964, pp. 1, 16.

[37]*Public Papers of the Presidents of the United States. Lyndon B. Johnson, 1965* (Washington: USGPO, 1966), pp. 281-87.

[38]Benne and Hefner, *Defining America*, pp. 120-40.

[39]Trueblood, *The Future of the Christian*, pp. 81, 86, 88-89.

[40]Ibid., pp. 93-94, 102.

Chapter Five

[1]Text of the statement by Senator Hatfield reprinted in *Between a Rock*, p. 94.

[2]Billy Graham, *Can the Tide Be Turned?* (Minneapolis: BGEA, 1976), p. 15.

[3]Walfred Peterson, "The Case Against Civil Religion," *Eternity*, 24 (Oct. 1973), 23.

[4]Ibid.

[5]Sermon preached at the National Presbyterian Church, Washington, D.C., on May 20, 1973, reprinted in the *Congressional Record*, Vol. 119, Pt. 13 (May 24, 1973), 16924-25. This attitude is perfectly exemplified by an experience which the *New York Times* religion editor reported having at Campus Crusade's EXPLO '72. He ran into a man selling Jesus bumper stickers and American flag decals and asked him: "Why both?" The man replied: "I figure that a good Christian is a good American and vice versa." Edward B. Fiske, "Corralling Jesus in the Cotton

Bowl," *Saturday Review*, 55 (July 8, 1972), 20.

⁶Valentine, "Civil Religion," p. 48.

⁷Cotham, *Politics*, p. 166.

⁸Martin E. Marty, *The New Shape of American Religion* (New York: Harper & Row, 1959), pp. 37-39.

⁹Donald B. Kraybill, *Our Star-Spangled Faith* (Scottdale, Pa.: Herald Press, 1976), p. 177.

¹⁰Callender, *Congressional Record*, Vol. 119, Pt. 13 (May 24, 1973), p. 16926.

¹¹Speech by Mark O. Hatfield, "Christian Citizens Confronting Civil Religion," *Proceedings of the Christian Life Commission Seminar "Christian Citizenship '76," Washington, D.C., March 22-24, 1976*, ed. Foy Valentine (Nashville: Christian Life Commission, SBC, 1976), pp. 71-72.

¹²Peterson, "Case Against Civil Religion," p. 27.

¹³Jim Wallis, *Agenda for Biblical People* (New York: Harper & Row, 1976), p. 43.

¹⁴Miller, *Piety along the Potomac*, p. 44.

¹⁵The implications of these two examples of civil religiosity are examined in Richard V. Pierard, "The Golden Image of Nebuchadnezzar," *Reformed Journal*, 22 (Dec. 1972), 9-13. Recognizing the difficulties caused by his role in Honor America Day, Graham assured an interviewer a few years later that his Bicentennial activity would not be open to the critique that he equated Christianity with America or American values. Gerald S. Strober, *GRAHAM: A Day in Billy's Life* (Garden City, N.Y.: Doubleday, 1976), p. 59.

¹⁶Reported by Wes Michaelson, "NAE in Washington: Bicentennial Faith," *Sojourners*, 5 (Mar. 1976), pp. 8-10.

¹⁷Hibbs, *White House Sermons*, p. vi.

¹⁸Ibid., pp. 56, 68.

¹⁹Quoted in MacKay, *Heritage and Destiny*, p. 81.

²⁰(New Brunswick, N.J.: Rutgers University Press, 1957), p. vii.

²¹Herman Melville, *White-Jacket, or, The World in a Man-of-War* (Boston: Page, 1892 [c. 1850]), p. 144.

²²Clinton Rossiter, "The American Mission," *American Scholar*, 20 (Winter 1950-51), 19-20. For a fairly positive assessment of the role of Protestant religious thinking in the development of a sense of national mission, see Clouse, *Millennialism and America*, pp. 35-53.

²³John Warwick Montgomery, *The Shaping of America* (Minneapolis: Bethany Fellowship, 1976), p. 115.

²⁴Rogers, *Let Freedom Ring!*, pp. 21-22.

²⁵Josiah Strong, *Our Country* (Cambridge: Harvard University Press, 1963 [c. 1886]), pp. 200-02, 214-15.

²⁶Sermon of May 15, 1898, quoted in John E. Smylie, "Protestant Clergymen and America's World Role, 1865-1900," Diss. Princeton Theological Seminary, 1959, p. 459.

²⁷*New York Times*, July 7, 1898, p. 1.

²⁸James F. Rusling, "Interview with President McKinley," *Christian Advocate*, 78 (Jan. 22, 1903), 137.

²⁹*New York Times*, July 11, 1898, p. 10.

³⁰Winthrop S. Hudson, *Religion in America* (New York: Scribner's, 1973), pp. 112-14.

³¹Mark O. Hatfield, "Civil Religion," *Evangelical Visitor*, 86 (Aug. 10, 1973), 4.

³²D. James Kennedy, pastor of Coral Ridge Presbyterian Church, Fort Lauderdale, Florida, writing in the *Presbyterian Journal*, 31 (Nov. 22, 1972), 7-8.

³³Norman Vincent Peale, *One Nation Under God* (Pawling, N.Y.: Foundation for

Christian Living, 1972), pp. 3, 6-7.

[34]Rogers, *Let Freedom Ring!*, pp. 19-20.

[35]George Otis, *The Solution to Crisis-America* (Old Tappan, N.J.: Revell, 1972), p. 53.

[36]Tim LaHaye, *The Bible's Influence on American History* (San Diego: Master Books, 1976), p. 9.

[37]Edward L. R. Elson, "The Source of Our Life," *Decision*, No. 10 (July 1969), p. 3. The most detailed discussion of Christian principles that allegedly underlay the founding of the United States may be found in two textbooks which are widely used in Christian parochial schools: Verna M. Hall, *Christian History of the Constitution of the United States of America* (1962), and Rosalie J. Slater, *Teaching and Learning America's Christian History* (1965). Privately printed, they are distributed by the Foundation for American Christian Education, San Francisco, California 94132. Peter Marshall and David Manuel in their book *The Light and the Glory* (Old Tappan, N.J.: Revell, 1977) develop in considerable detail the thesis that God chose America to be a shining example for the remainder of the world and that he intervened repeatedly in the nation's early history to achieve his intended purpose.

[38]James C. Hefley, *America: One Nation Under God* (Wheaton: Victor Books, 1972), p. 15.

[39]"Editorial: God Bless America," *Decision*, No. 16 (Apr. 1975), p. 2.

[40]Stephen Strang, "God's Hand in Our History," *Christian Life*, 37 (Jan. 1976), 24.

[41]Lambert C. Mims, *For Christ and Country* (Old Tappan, N.J.: Revell, 1969), pp. 92-95. Robert N. Schaper, in a sermon published in the Fuller Evangelistic Association organ, *Today's Christian*, No. 7 (July 1976), pp. 1-2, contends "there are values and ideas" in the Declaration of Independence "that are very precious to anyone who takes the Christian gospel seriously." After singling out seven of these, he compares American freedom with that found in Christ and concludes with an invitation statement affirming the excellence of the former but conceding the superiority of the latter.

[42]A description of the Muhlenberg incident is contained in William H. Lazareth, ed., *The Left Hand of God: Essays on Discipleship and Patriotism* (Philadelphia: Fortress, 1976), p. xiii. Graham made this historical observation in a speech at a White House prayer breakfast. *New York Times*, Oct. 23, 1969, p. 32; and Henderson, *Nixon Theology*, p. 12. A more balanced view of evangelical participation in the conflict is Mark A. Noll, *Christians in the American Revolution* (Grand Rapids: Eerdmans, 1977).

[43]Derek Prince, *Shaping History Through Prayer and Fasting* (Old Tappan, N.J.: Revell, 1973), p. 40; and "The American Dream," *Radio Bible Class Discovery Digest* (Grand Rapids), No. 1 (July 1976), 8.

[44]LaHaye, *Bible's Influence on American History*, p. 35.

[45]Robert Flood, *America: God Shed His Grace on Thee* (Chicago: Moody, 1975), pp. 164-65; and Harry Van't Kerkhoff, *1776 to 1976: Reflections on America's Past and the Future* (Westchester, Ill.: Good News Publishers, 1975), p. 4.

[46]John F. DeVries, *The Light to See: A Bicentennial Prayer and Bible Study* (South Holland, Ill.: World Home Bible League, 1974), p. 86.

[47]Flood, *America*, pp. 114-15, 129.

[48]The theme of godly America and its apostasy is also treated in Richard V. Pierard, "Evangelicals and the Bicentennial," *Reformed Journal*, 26 (Oct. 1976), 19-23.

[49]Jimmy and Carol Owens, *If My People . . . : A Handbook for National Intercession* (Waco: Word, 1974), p. 89.

[50]Rus Walton, *One Nation Under God* (Old Tappan, N.J.: Revell, 1975), pp. 44, 46.

[51]Graham, *Can the Tide Be Turned?*, pp. 10-12.

[52]Flood, *America*, p. 152.

[53]Charles E. Blair, *Americans Speak Out* (Chicago: Moody, 1972), p. 96.

[54]See Pierard, "Evangelicals and the Bicentennial," pp. 19-20.

[55]George Otis, *The Blueprint* (Van Nuys, Calif.: Bible Voice, 1975), pp. 190-91.

[56]Montgomery, *Shaping of America*, p. 51. Historian David Gill provides a concise, well-balanced survey of the religious views of the nation's founders in his essay "Faith of the Founding Fathers?" *A Nation Under God?* ed. C. E. Gallivan (Waco: Word, 1976), pp. 25-45.

[57]Walton, *One Nation Under God*, pp. 21, 16.

[58]This point is made by Roger Dewey, "Power and Politics," *Inside*, No. 7 (Feb.-Apr. 1976), pp. 6-7.

[59]Priscilla Luther, "America: One Nation Under God?" *Christian Patriot*, 31 (Sept. 1975), 2-3, calls attention to this.

[60]Bellah, "Civil Religion in America," pp. 18-19.

[61]Mark O. Hatfield, speech delivered at the Annual Conference of the United Methodist Church, Baltimore, June 4, 1976. Text in possession of the authors.

[62]Hatfield, *Between a Rock*, p. 101.

[63]Garth M. Rosell, "The Spirit of '76 and the Voice of the Prophet," *Bethel Seminary Journal*, 20 (Spring 1972), 21.

Chapter Six

[1]For the New Testament usage of the term *saints* as the people of God, see Rom. 1:7; 8:27;12:13; 1 Cor. 1:2; 16:1; and Jude 3. In the first five chapters we have tried to present in a relatively detached and scholarly fashion the history of civil religion and to point out its positive and negative aspects. Now, in this final chapter we intend to put forth our own reactions to American civil religion and to challenge our fellow evangelicals to come to grips with the dangers we believe it holds for the Christian faith.

[2]John Milton, *Works*, F. A. Patterson, ed. (New York: Columbia University Press, 1931-34), IV, 340.

[3]Owen, "Christ's Kingdom and the Magistrate's Power," p. 381.

[4]For examples, see Donald G. Bloesch, *The Evangelical Renaissance* (Grand Rapids: Eerdmans, 1973); Richard Quebedeaux, *The Young Evangelicals* (New York: Harper & Row, 1974); and "Born Again: The Year of the Evangelicals," *Newsweek*, 88 (Oct. 25, 1976), 68-78.

[5]Examples of this stance may be found in the titles referred to in chapter five, notes 33-38, 45, 50, 55, as well as Jack Wyrtzen, *America: Wake Up Or Blow Up!* (Schroon Lake, N.Y.: Word of Life Fellowship, 1976); Billy James Hargis, *Why I Fight for a Christian America* (Nashville: Thomas Nelson, 1974); S. Franklin Logsdon, *Is the U.S.A. in Prophecy?*, rev. ed. (Grand Rapids: Zondervan, 1974); and Benjamin Weiss, *God in American History: A Documentation of America's Religious Heritage*, rev. ed. (South Pasadena, Calif.; National Educators Fellowship, 1975). The list is virtually inexhaustible.

[6]Justice William O. Douglas, majority opinion in *Zorach v. Clauson*, 343 U.S. 313 (1951).

[7]Quoted in Ronald Wells, "The Meaning of America," *Inside*, No. 7 (Feb.-Apr. 1976), p. 46. Compare this with a Bicentennial-year letter-to-the-editor by an angry Kansan: "People have made (or are in the process of making) millions of dollars by writing about a convicted murderer's clan, exposing the sexual promiscuity during the life of a president now dead, or explaining their part in this nation's worst scandal. Others have paid (or are in the process of paying) millions

of dollars in bribes to obtain contracts for their companies. There are even those who willingly sell their grain to our supposed enemies. I suggest we accept reality and, in this our Bicentennial year, change our national motto from 'In God We Trust' to 'Anything for a Buck.' " *Topeka Daily Capital,* Mar. 20, 1976, p. 4.

[8]For a detailed discussion and refutation of this view, see Robert D. Linder and Richard V. Pierard, *Politics: A Case for Christian Action* (Downers Grove, Ill.: InterVarsity, 1973).

[9]Bill Bright, Keynote Speech at the Summit Conference of Church Leaders for Prayer for the Nation, Chicago, Sept. 12-13, 1975. Tape in possession of the authors.

[10]Ibid.

[11]Jim Wallis and Wes Michaelson, "The Plan to Save America," *Sojourners,* 5 (Apr. 1976), pp. 5-12; "Politics from the Pulpit," *Newsweek,* 88 (Sept. 6, 1976), pp. 49, 51; and Interview with Bill Bright, "Yoking Politics and Proclamation—Can It Be Done?" *Christianity Today,* 20 (Sept. 24, 1976), pp. 20-22.

[12]Interview with Ronald Reagan, "Reagan Seeks Return to Absolutes," *National Courier,* 1 (Aug. 6, 1976), p. 6.

[13]Callahan, "The New Pluralism," pp. 527-31.

[14]For an example of this viewpoint, see Graham, *Can the Tide Be Turned?,* p. 14.

[15]The other side of this ideological coin is, of course, a discussion of the virtues of civic culture and its relationship to evangelical faith. Then the crucial question becomes, Can culture be "Christian" rather than, Is the civil religion "ersatz"? Once again, there are legitimate differences of opinion over to what extent—if any—a culture can be Christianized. Certainly evangelical Christianity can and has exercised a determinative cultural influence over certain societies in the past. But does that mean that any society has or can possess a distinctively "Christian culture" or can we speak only of cultures deeply influenced by Christian values? It is not the purpose of this book to provide answers to this important question even though much of what we say in chapter six will be suggestive of our position on the matter. For examples of two very different points of view on the biblical Christian stance toward civic culture, see the radical evangelical magazine *Sojourners* (published monthly in Washington, D.C.) and the literature produced by the Toronto-based and Dooyeweerdian-oriented Institute for Christian Studies.

[16]*Congressional Record,* Vol. 120, Pt. 9 (Apr. 30, 1974), 12274.

[17]Hatfield, *Between a Rock,* pp. 100-01.

[18]For a discussion of this matter in a slightly different context, see Robert D. Linder, "Civil Religion and Baptist Responsibility," *Southwestern Journal of Theology,* 18 (Spring 1976), 25-39.

[19]This charge was leveled by Celsus in his book *True Discourse* written about A.D. 180 and largely preserved in Origen's refutation of it in his *Against Celsus.* See Origen, *Contra Celsum,* ed. and trans. Henry Chadwick (Cambridge: University Press, 1965), pp. 7-8.

[20]For a fuller discussion of this topic see Neuhaus, *Time Toward Home;* and Hayes, *Essays on Nationalism,* pp. 6-7.

[21]Material for this section is taken mostly from Richard V. Pierard, "Positive Patriotism," *Vanguard* (Toronto), July-Aug. 1976, pp. 10-12. See also Neuhaus, "Patriotism and Puritans," pp. 4-5; Martin E. Marty, "Vice and Virtue: Our Moral Condition," *Time,* 106 (Oct. 27, 1975), pp. 82-84; William H. Lazareth, "Sentinels for the Tricentennial," in Lazareth, ed., *The Left Hand of God,* pp. 156-67; and Lee E. Snook, "Piety and Patriotism: The Dilemma of the Christian Citizen," *Preaching on National Holidays,* ed. M. Motter (Philadelphia: Fortress, 1976), pp. 75-81.

[22]George Sweeting, "America, Right or Wrong?" *Moody Monthly*, 74 (July-Aug. 1974), 4.

[23]Cited in Marty, "Vice and Virtue," p. 82.

[24]C. Welton Gaddy, *Profile of a Christian Citizen* (Nashville: Broadman, 1974), p. 48.

[25]Quoted in Walden Howard, "The Challenge of the Bicentennial," *Faith at Work*, 89 (Feb. 1976), p. 7.

[26]Cited approvingly in Rogers, *Let Freedom Ring!*, pp. 14-15. For similar statements of pietistic jingoism concerning the virtues of recent presidents, see John S. Bonnell, *Presidential Profiles: Religion in the Life of the American Presidents* (Philadelphia: Westminster, 1971), pp. 229, 244.

[27]Henry, "Reflections on a Nation in Transition," p. 57.

[28]Many other nations currently are socially fragmented and experience a high degree of political polarization. However, America suffers far more from this sort of thing because of its size, its increasingly pluralistic ethnic and religious composition and its advanced state of technology which tends to exacerbate this condition. For a recent suggestion to decriminalize murder, see Joseph P. McGrath, "The Case for Decriminalizing Murder," *National Review*, 28 (Oct. 1, 1976), 1066-67.

[29]Orlando E. Costas, *The Church and Its Mission: A Shattering Critique From the Third World* (Wheaton: Tyndale, 1974), p. 14.

[30]Billy Graham, "Why Lausanne?" *Christianity Today*, 18 (Sept. 13, 1974), p. 7. Also see John Stott, *The Lausanne Covenant* (Minneapolis: World Wide, 1974), p. 30; and Ronald J. Sider, ed., *The Chicago Declaration* (Carol Stream, Ill.: Creation House, 1974), p. 2.

[31]Cited in Simpson, *Puritanism in Old and New England*, p. 97.

[32]For an indication of the magnitude of the problem which evangelical Christians in America now face and some hints concerning how they can proceed to deal with it, see Richard J. Mouw, *Politics and the Biblical Drama* (Grand Rapids: Eerdmans, 1976); and Isaac C. Rottenberg, "The Shape of the Church's Social-Economic Witness," *Reformed Journal*, 27 (May 1977), 16-21.

[33]Mark O. Hatfield, "Celebrating the Year of Liberation," *Christianity Today*, 20 (Mar. 26, 1976), 13.

Selected Reading List

This is not an exhaustive bibliography. Even if it pretended to be, it would be out of date by the time this volume was published, for studies of civil religion are pouring from the presses at an extraordinary rate of speed, and interest in the topic shows no signs of abatement. In addition to the titles mentioned below we recommend that the reader who wishes to pursue seriously the study of civil religion examine our footnotes for further direction. This selected reading list is simply a guide for the beginner.

Inclusion of an item does not necessarily imply our endorsement of its contents. An asterisk (*) denotes those books available in paperback.

Ahlstrom, Sydney E. *A Religious History of the American People.* New Haven: Yale University Press, 1972.*

Anderson, John B. *Vision and Betrayal in America.* Waco: Word Books, 1975.

Bellah, Robert N. and McLoughlin, William G., eds. *Religion in America.* Boston: Houghton Mifflin, 1968.*

Cherry, Conrad. *God's New Israel: Religious Interpretations of American Destiny.* Englewood Cliffs, N.J.: Prentice-Hall, 1971.*

Clouse, Robert G.; Linder, Robert D.; and Pierard, Richard V., eds. *The Cross and the Flag.* Carol Stream, Ill.: Creation House, 1972.*

Cotham, Perry C. *Politics, Americanism, and Christianity.* Grand Rapids: Baker Book House, 1976.

Deweese, Charles and Tonks, A. Ronald. *Faith, Stars, and Stripes: The Impact of Christianity on the Life History of America.* Nashville: Broadman, 1976.

Handy, Robert T. *A Christian America: Protestant Hopes and Historical Realities.* New York: Oxford University Press, 1971.*

Hart, R. P. *The Political Pulpit.* West Lafayette, Ind.: Purdue University Press, 1977.*

Hatfield, Mark O. *Between a Rock and a Hard Place.* Waco: Word Books, 1976.*

Jones, Donald G. and Richey, Russell E., eds. *American Civil Religion.* New York: Harper & Row, 1974.*

Linder, Robert D. and Pierard, Richard V. *Politics: A Case for Christian Action.* Downers Grove, Ill.: InterVarsity Press, 1973.*

McLoughlin, William G., ed. *The American Evangelicals, 1800-1900.* New York: Harper & Row, 1968.*

Marty, Martin E. *A Nation of Behavers.* Chicago: University of Chicago Press, 1976.

Mead, Sidney E. *The Nation With the Soul of a Church.* New York: Harper & Row, 1975.*

Mead, Sidney E. *The Old Religion in the Brave New World: Reflections on the Relation Between Christendom and the Republic.* Berkeley: University of California Press, 1977.

Menendez, Albert J. *Religion at the Polls.* Philadelphia: Westminster, 1977.*

Moltmann, Jürgen, et. al. *Religion and Political Society.* New York: Harper & Row, 1974.*

Monsma, Stephen. *The Unraveling of America.* Downers Grove, Ill.: InterVarsity Press, 1974.*

Montgomery, John Warwick. *The Shaping of America.* Minneapolis: Bethany Fellowship, 1976.

Neuhaus, Richard J. *Time Toward Home: The American Experiment as Revelation.* New York: Seabury, 1975.

Pierard, Richard V. *The Unequal Yoke: Evangelical Christianity and Political*

    Conservatism. Philadelphia: Lippincott, 1970.*

Skillen, James, ed. *Christian Politics: False Hope* or *Biblical Demand?* Indiana, Pa.: Jubilee Enterprises, 1976.*

Smith, Elwyn A. *The Religion of the Republic*. Philadelphia: Fortress Press, 1970.

Stringfellow, William. *An Ethic for Christians and Other Aliens in a Strange Land*. Waco: Word Books, 1973.

Strout, Cushing. *The New Heavens and New Earth: Political Religion in America*. New York: Harper & Row, 1974.*

Trueblood, D. Elton. *Abraham Lincoln: Theologian of American Anguish*. New York: Harper & Row, 1973.

Tuveson, Ernest L. *Redeemer Nation: The Idea of America's Millennial Role*. Chicago: University of Chicago Press, 1968.*

Van Allen, Rodger, ed. *American Religious Values and the Future of America*, Philadelphia: Fortress, 1977.

Wallis, Jim. *Agenda for Biblical People*. New York: Harper & Row, 1976.*

Wells, David F. and Woodbridge, John D., eds. *The Evangelicals*. Rev. ed., Grand Rapids: Baker, 1977.*

The entire issue of the following periodicals was devoted to the subject of civil religion.

Africa Today, 23 (Oct.—Dec. 1976).

Fides et Historia, 8 (Spring 1975).

Journal of Theology for Southern Africa, No. 19, June 1977.

Religious Education, 70 (Sept.-Oct. 1975).

NAME AND SUBJECT INDEX

BIBLICAL REFERENCES